WEIGHT TRAINING
FOR WOMEN

WEIGHT TRAINING FOR WOMEN

Mary Southall and E. G. Bartlett

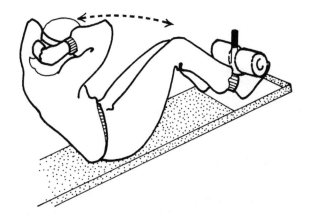

David & Charles
Newton Abbot   London   North Pomfret (Vt)

British Library Cataloguing in Publication Data

Southall, Mary
  Weight training for women.
  1. Weight lifting for women.
  I. Title   II. Bartlett, E. G.
  796.4'1   GV546.6.W64

ISBN 0–7153–8842–8

Phototypeset by Photo·Graphics
and printed in Great Britain
by Redwood Burn Ltd, Trowbridge
for David & Charles Publishers plc
Brunel House Newton Abbot Devon

Published in the United States of America
by David & Charles Inc
North Pomfret Vermont 05053 USA

Contents

Acknowledgements

The authors gratefully acknowledge the help and advice freely given by Lynda C. Spear, IHBC (International Health and Beauty Council Credits), FETC (Further Education Teacher's Certificate Credit), WFBB (Welsh Federation of Body Builders), Miss Wales 1982 and 1983, and by Andrea McKim, British Amateur Athletics Board Club Coach, who holds sixteen athletic awards and is currently Instructor at Fairwater Leisure Centre, Cardiff.

Introduction

For many years, weight training was considered a man's activity, but of recent years women have become more and more involved. A few go in for body building or weight-lifting in the same way as men do, but generally women are more concerned with general fitness, figure trimming, slimming, correcting faults in their early development, or with supplementing their training for other sports or athletics. There are still other ways in which weight training can help them. The exercises will overcome tired feelings, will tone up the muscles, will help to cope with backache during pregnancy and with recovering the figure after childbirth. All these uses of weight training will be looked at and suitable training schedules detailed, as well as warming-up exercises not involving the use of weights.

First of all, what we mean by weight training should be defined. Weight training is using weights, in the form of barbells or dumb-bells, to tone up or develop the muscles. It must not be confused with weight-lifting or power-lifting, which are sports in which contestants strive to lift the heaviest possible weights in competition lifts. Today, many weight trainers do not use the sets of loose weights that are in sports shops, but go to a leisure centre, where machines allow you to do similar exercises, working against resistance. Whether you choose to buy a set of weights and train in the privacy of your own home or go to a leisure centre and use the apparatus there is a matter of personal choice, and will be dictated by the time and money available, as well as by other considerations. In every routine given here suitable exercises are given for use at home or in a leisure centre.

Women have for too long been referred to disparagingly as 'the weaker sex'. When we consider how much more they have to do than men, running a home, often with a full-time job as well, having children, caring for them, cleaning, cooking, shopping, and a thousand other tasks, we may well feel that they are really the stronger sex. Yet, taking size for size, a woman is not generally as strong physically as a man, and the exercises she should take will therefore differ from those appropriate to a man training for the same end. In particular, women must be wary of overhead lifts until they have strengthened their back muscles by gentle exercises first.

The form of training differs according to the purpose in view. Thus, for simply keeping fit or toning up the muscles, a regular routine that covers all the muscle groups in turn will suffice. To build up any muscle or the body as a whole, you must follow a routine that involves working until you just cannot do another repetition. To build up the body if you are underweight or undersized, exercise must be combined with an increase in protein in the diet. To reduce, light exercise must be combined with a decrease in calorie intake. To aid you in your particular sport, exercises must be chosen to develop the muscles you need and at the same time build your stamina without slowing you down or making you muscle-bound. All these matters will be taken into account in this book.

The work is divided into three sections. In Section 1, the background knowledge necessary for the most effective training is given. Different types of apparatus are discussed, along with the basic principles, the structure of the human body, the muscle groups, diets to help you, the psychology of training and the benefits of relaxation. Do not pass over this section in your eagerness to start training – it is vital to your understanding of what you are doing.

In Section 2, each of the exercises is described simply, with diagrams, covering all those you can do at home, either with or without apparatus, and going on to those you can do at leisure centres with the apparatus available there. Although all the exercises are grouped together in this section, this is done for ease of reference only, and you should on no account try to work through them all. You should first read on to Section 3, where you will find schedules suitable for different purposes. Decide why you want to do weight training, turn to the appropriate chapter, and there you will find what to do. It may need to be combined with one of the diets in Section 1.

Section 1

GENERAL

1 Apparatus

The apparatus you will need for weight training can be as simple or as complex as you like to make it, and will in part be dictated by how much money you are prepared to spend. You can manage with a pair of dumb-bells, but it is better if you can also add a barbell and a bench, because these will give you a greater variety of exercises to make your training more interesting. Simply repeating the same exercises can become boring and this can sap your resolve to continue. If you want to use expensive machines, it is probably best to begin your training in a leisure centre or commercial gymnasium where this apparatus is available. You can then see how you get on with it before rushing into a large outlay of capital.

Assuming you are planning to train at home and have no apparatus, the first piece to consider buying is a pair of dumb-bells. There are two kinds: those made of metal or heavy plastic of a fixed weight, and those that consist of a short rod with collars that enable you to slip disc weights on to either side, holding them in position by screwing down collars. The latter are better, as they will enable you to increase the weight you are using, as your strength increases, and so will give you progressively increasing resistance to work against – an essential factor if you want to develop muscle. In the early days of weight training, the weights on dumb-bells or barbells consisted of hollow metal spheres into which lead shot could be poured to increase the weight being lifted. Today, there are similar ones into which wet or dry sand can be poured to increase the weight. Since either of these alternatives would involve weighing the dumb-bells to see what weight you were actually lifting, it

is better to buy the type in which you simply slide on extra disc weights. These are labelled either in pounds or kilograms, and are so graduated that you can increase the weight you are using by as little as 1lb or ½kg.

The next piece of equipment you should consider buying is a barbell. This consists of a bar, approximately 5 or 6ft long, with two collars either end which you can screw down to hold disc weights in position. The inner collars are tightly screwed equidistant from either end and about 6in from the ends. Disc weights are then slipped on to make up the desired weight. The outer collars are now added to hold these weights in position, and screwed down tightly. You must of course balance the weight on either side, and make sure that the collars are firm, so that the weights will not slide inwards to trap your hands, or fall off on your toes.

Often dumb-bells and barbells are sold together as a set. The disc weights with them will then fit either the barbell rod or the dumb-bell rods. The cost is dictated by the total poundage you buy. You can get sets as low as 50lb or go up to several hundred pounds. It is best to start with the lower range and then buy more weights as you need them. If your rods are of a standard thickness, this is easy, but be wary because some manufacturers have made their rods of a slightly different thickness so that only their weights will fit them. This limits you to going back to the same firm for extra discs. Athough pounds are used in this book, some firms are labelling their weights in kilograms. If you are using kilograms it is simple to make the necessary conversions.

The cost of even such simple apparatus as described above can be as much as £1 per 1lb weight, but second-hand sets can often be seen advertised in the body-building magazines or in *Exchange and Mart* and of course these are just as good, but make sure before you buy anything that the collars fit and grip tightly, and that they are not rusty. Collars tighten by screwing down a peg or by using an Alan key.

To add further variety to the exercises you can do at home, consider next getting a bench. This can be a simple flat bench about 18in from the floor, long enough to support your buttocks, back, head and shoulders, with your feet on the floor off one end. An ordinary wooden household bench is quite serviceable; if you want something more elaborate, padded ones of tubular steel are available in sports shops, as are adjustable ones which enable the top to be set at various angles.

With these three pieces of apparatus, you are ready to start home training, but even if you have only got dumb-bells, do not worry, because you will see in Chapters 10 and 11 that for every barbell exercise there is a corresponding one with dumb-bells, so you can easily make substitutions in your routines and develop the same muscles.

If you want to add further to your home equipment, the next purchase is a pair of iron boots. These are metal plates which you strap to the soles of your own shoes, and they have a rod projecting either side, to which you can fit disc weights, holding them in position with a screw collar as you do on the dumb-bells. Thus you can add to the weight on your feet when doing exercises for leg or abdominal development. Heavy boots would be a good substitute if you do not wish to buy the iron ones.

A wrist roller is another useful piece of equipment. This is a short rod usually of wood with a cord attached to the centre. On this cord you hang weights, and you turn the rod to wind them up by the cord. It is such a simple design that you could make one for yourself out of a piece of broomstick 1ft long.

Many people today turn to rowing machines or exercise bikes for their workouts. The rowing machine consists of a sliding seat, a foot rest and two handles which you pull against the resistance of springs in a simulation of rowing a boat. It

exercises the same muscles as rowing on a lake or on the sea would do. The exercise bike is really a static bicycle. You sit on the saddle, hold the handlebars and pedal, the resistance of the pedals, which is adjustable, providing the exercise. These bikes have a resistance indicator, a timer and a speed meter to show how fast you are going. It is usual to cycle for a set time against a set resistance, and to increase either the time or the resistance or both as you progress. The benefits are similar to cycling, and you have to balance the absence of traffic hazards against the fact that you lose the advantages of being in the open air and getting somewhere.

If you decide to train at a leisure centre, you may find that they give you the option of using loose weights on dumb-bell and barbell rods such as we have described above, but you are more likely to find that they have machines. These have the advantage that the weights cannot fall out and injure you since they move on runners, and you can change the weight you are using more easily, since you simply insert a pin at the weight level that you want. The machines generally found at leisure centres or commercial gyms are called 'Stations', and you will normally find the following fifteen stations:

1 **Leg Press Station** This is a padded seat with a back rest, on a metal bar. It has resistance foot rests attached to an adjustable weight stack.

2 **Hip Flexor Station** A steel frame with a padded back, arm supports and hand grips. It is fitted at a suitable height to allow floor clearance when you are supported on your forearms.

3 **Thigh and Knee Leg Extension Station** A padded bench with foot rollers connected to an adjustable weight stack.

4 **High Pulley Station** A curved bar with handgrips, connected by cable to a high pulley and weight stack.

5 **Rowing Station** A weight stack attached to low cables and stirrup handles. It has a padded seat and foot rests.

6 **Low Pulley Thigh Pulls Station** A foot strap and cable attached to a floor level pulley and weight stack.

11

7 **Dead Lift Station** An arrangement of weights on runners attached to the wall, with handles to raise.

8 **Abdominal Conditioner Sit-ups Station** A padded board adjustable to several angles, with foot rollers.

9 **Chest Press Station** A padded bench or stool, with metal lifting arm and hand grips attached to a weight stack.

10 **Chest Bench Station** A seat with arm resistance pads at shoulder height, attached to an adjustable weight stack.

11 **Leg Squat Station** This consists of two shoulder pads attached to a resistance lifting bar and adjustable weight stack.

12 **Dipping Station** A low metal support with rail and hand grips.

13 **Chinning Station** A high metal support, with rail and hand grips.

14 **Standing Twister** A circular turntable platform, attached to a handrail at shoulder height.

15 **Seated Twister** A circular turntable seat with a foot rest attached to a waist level handrail.

Sometimes, several of these machines will be incorporated in one piece of apparatus, standing centrally, and you will be able to move around it, doing one exercise on one side and another on another. Such multi-gyms, as they are called, can also be bought for home use, but they are rather expensive and of course they take up a considerable amount of room.

As well as leisure centres run by local authorities, there are an increasing number of commercial gyms. Most of these are very well equipped, and as well as all the apparatus listed above they will have showers, saunas and other extras. Before joining one, however, it would be wise to pay a visit to see how it is being run. Is there a qualified instructor in attendance? If so, will you have to follow a set course which she or he prescribes? Is instruction on an individual or class basis?

To get the best out of weight training, individual courses need to be prescribed for your individual needs. You may not get this in a class. You need an instructor in whom you have confidence and with whom you get on well. Find out all these things before you commit yourself. Further considerations on the relative merits of where to train are given in Chapters 2 and 7.

2 Basic Principles

There are various factors to be taken into account when deciding your choice of apparatus and training venue. In order to build up muscle, you need to train three nights a week, with a night off between sessions. Thus you would train Monday, Wednesday and Friday, or Tuesday, Thursday and Saturday, but not both. If on the other hand you simply want to keep fit, light exercises can be done every day.

This raises the point – will a leisure centre be open on the nights you want to go? Will they have organised classes on some of those nights? Would you be able to follow your own individual course? If the cost of using the machines at a leisure centre is £1 to £1.50 per evening, will you not find it more expensive in the long run than buying a set of weights and training at home?

Added to this, there is the question of time and travelling. If the nearest centre is some miles from your home, petrol or bus fares must be taken into account. Centres will be open at fixed hours, and you may have to book in advance. Some are crowded and it is very difficult to get in.

Finally, there is the consideration that some will have separate nights for women and others will not. If they do have separate nights, you may find that the males have the advantage, and the ladies are restricted to one night a week. If there were mixed nights, would you feel happy if you turned out to be the only woman training in a room full of men?

If you train at home, you can pick the hours and nights to suit yourself. You will not have to travel, which on cold winter nights can be a deterrent. You may be able to involve husband or big brother, and get them to lose some flab as well. And when you have finished, you could sell your apparatus second-hand, and your total expenditure on training would then work out less than a year at a leisure centre.

On the other hand, the advantages of going to a centre are threefold. First, they have all the apparatus, much of it modern and sophisticated and completely outside the price range that an ordinary person could contemplate buying, even if there were room in the house to set it up. Secondly, because all the weights run on rollers and they cannot fall out on you, the machines are safer to use, though it should be emphasized that with ordinary care in screwing collars down tightly, there is nothing dangerous in dumb-bells and barbell. Thirdly, you will meet other enthusiasts at a leisure centre, who will give you plenty of encouragement. You may also pick up tips on training, and will be able to share experiences.

Leisure centres and commercial gyms are run in one of two ways. Either they have organised classes and perhaps private lessons as well, in which case you will have an instructor who will plan your course and guide you; or they are open for anyone who pays the fee simply to go along and use the apparatus that is available. In this case, you have to know what you are doing, though instruction on how to use each piece of equipment is usually displayed. You could follow any of the courses in this book on an, open night, providing you could go often enough. Do not fall into the trap of taking advice from all and sundry whom you meet there, however. Some may know less than you do about it. Do not try to compete in the weights you are using, but choose those appropriate for your own training schedule.

There are various questions you will want to ask before you embark on a course of training.

When Should You Train?

The answer depends on your purpose. As already mentioned, if you want to build muscle, three nights a week, with a night off in between. If you want to keep fit or do lighter exercises, every day would be appropriate, with perhaps one day off a week to prevent your getting stale. If you want to improve your performance at some other sport or at athletics, then two nights a week in between your training sessions for your sport would be adequate. Train regularly at the same time each training night if possible, as this will get your body into a rhythm. The pattern will then become a habit that will in itself help you to keep going.

Consider that a full work-out as in Chapter 17 will take between one and a half and two hours, and the routines in the other chapters of Section 3 may take between ½ hour and 1 hour per session. You will then be able to set aside time at home or book your leisure centre evenings accordingly. You may train in the morning or the afternoon if this is more convenient to you than the evening, but do not do so within one and a half hours of a meal.

How Is Muscular Development Gained?

Building muscles is based on a simple physiological principle. Exercise breaks down muscular tissue, but Nature is a wonderful healer, and when repairing this breakdown she builds a little more, using the food and oxygen you take in to do so. Then, when you break down tissue again with further exercise, she builds a little extra again, and so your muscle grows.

Of course, there is a little more to it than that. You need the right intake of food; you need to consider general principles of health, as even minor disorders can upset your efforts. This, however, will be discussed later. The most important point about building muscle is that you must allow this rest period of forty-eight hours between sessions for Nature to make these repairs.

What Should You Wear When Training?

Loose clothing and the minimum of it is the answer. Your body needs to breathe, not only through your nose but also through your pores. Tight garments will restrict your movement which leads to your body pushing out against the restriction. The usual garments are shorts or loose trousers and a T-shirt although some girls prefer leotard and tights. At home it is a matter of choice. In some leisure centres or commercial gyms a track suit is insisted upon, since you will perspire freely when exercising.

Between exercises you should put on something warm so that you do not chill off. It is essential to wear comfortable shoes with a heel when you handle weights. Failure to wear shoes with a heel can lead to flat feet, but of course it must be a normal low one, not a high heel. Choose shoes that will not slip but have a firm grip on the floor. You may also find ankle socks comfortable.

What Are The Best Training Conditions?

A warm though not hot room, with plenty of fresh air and no distracting influences. Train with the window open. If you are training seriously for sport or for body building, it is better not to have the wireless on or taped music playing, as you need to concentrate on your exercises. Indeed, for muscular development this is absolutely essential, as by concentrating on the muscle you are using you can almost will it to grow. But, if you are simply training for suppleness or poise or to keep fit, and indeed in any course where the exercises are rhythmical, you may enjoy training to music.

You can of course train in your garden on the lawn if the weather is fine, but generally you will find that indoors is best. It helps to watch what you are doing in a full length mirror, to see that you are carrying out the movement correctly and to assist your concentration on the muscle group involved.

What Weights Should You Use?

There are two considerations here: what is your purpose in training and what is your body type? For simply keeping fit (Chapter 14), for slimming (Chapter 15), for suppleness and poise (Chapter 18) and for special conditions (Chapter 20), you will need very light weights, since rhythmic movement is used rather than the breaking down and rebuilding of muscle tissue. The weights to be used in circuit training (Chapter 19) or for athletics or sports (Chapter 21 and 22) are given in their respective chapters. But for building up your physique or any special muscle groups (Chapters 16 and 17), there is an easy way to work out the weight you must use. First, decide on your body type. Are you the thin, small-boned person? That is the ectomorphic type. Are you large, big-boned? That is the endomorphic type. Are you in between? That is the mesomorphic type. Having worked out your type, take each exercise you are going to do, in turn, load your dumb-bell or barbell with weights to the level where you can perform the exercise once only and that with some effort. The weight that you must use can be calculated as follows:

If you are an ectomorph use 60%.
If you are a mesomorph use 55%.
If you are an endomorph use 50%.

Formerly women used a slightly higher percentage, as men still do, but recently they have found that performing higher repetitions with a lighter weight yields better results. It may sound strange that the smaller-boned people should lift the heavier weights, for it is the big people who like lifting these. They can easily manage them and would prefer that to doing more repetitions with a lighter load. The thin people on the other hand are usually energetic types, and they would like to use a lighter weight and do more repetitions. If progress is to be achieved, however, each must stick to his type-training.

How Can You Assess Progress?

By taking your measurement and weight before and after, and at regular intervals in between. Do not expect too much too quickly. Muscular development takes time, and if you are aiming to build up your physique (Chapter 17) you can think in terms of a two-year course. Weigh yourself stripped and at the same time each week. Take the following measurements, or better still get someone to take them for you: height, neck, bust (normal), bust (when you

breathe in), waist, hips, upper arm (straight), upper arm (flexed), forearm, wrist, thigh, calf and ankle. Record all these measurements and your weight in a table, take them all a month later, and record those, and so on throughout your course. It is easy to rule up a suitable chart, and the progress you see on it will make your efforts seem worth while. If you are trying to slim, a weekly weight record is encouraging, but do not take it more often than that, as day to day variations are unimportant. It is the general tendency that matters.

You should see growth in a muscle in a couple of months, though if you are fat to begin with, you may actually see a decrease in some measurements as fat is got rid of before being replaced with firm hard muscle tissue. You should see progress in any slimming programme in a month or so.

Is There Anything Else To Be Taken Into Consideration?

Yes, total life style. Trimming your figure or building up your physique both demand attention to your diet. Chapters 5 and 6 will help you here.

Fresh air is important. Sleep with the window open. If you live in a city, try to get away from the pollution to the country or the seaside as often as possible. Aim at regular hours of sleep. Seven to eight hours is the normal requirement. Avoid drugs, smoking, alcohol and stimulants. If you have any medical condition such as heart or asthma, consult your doctor before embarking on a course of training.

Exercise will raise the rate of your heart beat, and you must stay within safe limits. Your normal pulse rate is just over 60. The safe limit is found by the formulae:
For beginners, 220 – your age × 60%.
For intermediate students, 220 – your age × 70%.
For experienced people, 220 – your age × 80%.
Top athletes have a lower pulse rate than most people, so can exert themselves more without passing the safe limit.

Finally, learn to relax (Chapter 8), and consider how psychology can help you get the maximum benefit from your training (Chapter 7).

When you come to the exercises, there are certain terms that are so commonly used it would be helpful to learn what they mean now.

Bar The long rod on which weights are loaded.

Barbell The rod when loaded.

Collar The screw-down disc that holds the weights in place.

Weights Sometimes called 'discs', these are the round weights with a hole in the middle that you fit onto the rods.

Dumb-bell rod The short rod that you load with weights.

Dumb-bell The rod when loaded.

Repetition The performance of an exercise once only.

Set A number of repetitions of one exercise.

Number of sets The number of times each set is to be performed.

Point of resistance The point in a series of repetitions where you just cannot do one more.

The last four terms are used to describe how often any particular exercise should be done. It is written thus: 3 × 10.

This means do 10 repetitions of the exercise, rest a minute, do 10 more, rest a minute, and do 10 more.

There could be anything from 1 to 5 sets.

If you are told, 'do 3 sets to the point of resistance', this means that in each of the 3 sets you go on until you just cannot do the last, taking the minute's rest between sets. It is this last repetition which you cannot manage that does the good.

3 The Female Body

Apart from the obvious ones arising out of being of a different sex, the female body has a number of slight differences to the male. The bones will be smaller and lighter; the cavity in the pelvis surrounded by hip bones will be wider; but the muscles are the same as a man's.

The body consists basically of a skeleton, which has 206 bones, supporting the muscles. There are over 600 muscles, the majority of which are attached to a bone either directly or by a tendon. Muscles are bundles of closely interlocking fibres; tendons are tough inelastic fibres. Within the rigid box formed by the skull is the brain. Within the torso lie organs such as the heart, lungs, liver, kidneys, etc. The heart, lungs and blood vessels take care of circulation and keep you alive; the digestive and excretory organs take care of food intake; sense organs give perceptions of the outside world.

It is unnecessary to have a comprehensive knowledge of anatomy in order to benefit from weight training, but you should be able to identify voluntary muscles so that you can develop them, and you should know your ideal weight and measurements. Your weight will depend on your height and on whether you are of the small, medium or large build (see the three types in the last chapter). The table below gives your ideal.

Ideally your weight should remain constant once you have reached the age of twenty-five, but many people do gain a little afterwards, reaching their maximum at about the age of fifty. In the case of an adult woman fat will account for twenty-five per cent of her weight. You will tend to put on fat around the upper arms and thighs, so these are the danger points to watch (see Diagram A on page 18).

The ideal figure for a woman seems to be one in which the bust is 1in less than the hips, and the waist 10in less than the bust, but fashions change, and these figures indicate aesthetically satisfying proportions rather than health or fitness. Child-bearing will alter them.

Height	Small Build	Medium Build	Large Build
4ft 10in	7st	7st 8lb	8st 6lb
4ft 11in	7st 3lb	7st 11lb	8st 9lb
5ft	7st 6lb	8st	8st 12lb
5ft 1in	7st 8lb	8st 4lb	9st 1lb
5ft 2in	7st 11lb	8st 8lb	9st 5lb
5ft 3in	8st	8st 12lb	9st 10lb
5ft 4in	8st 4lb	9st 2lb	9st 13lb
5ft 5in	8st 8lb	9st 4lb	10st 2lb
5ft 6in	8st 12lb	9st 9lb	10st 6lb
5ft 7in	9st 1lb	10st	10st 10lb
5ft 8in	9st 6lb	10st 4lb	11st
5ft 9in	9st 11lb	10st 8lb	11st 4lb
5ft 10in	10st 2lb	10st 11lb	11st 8lb
5ft 11in	10st 4lb	11st	11st 12lb
6ft	10st 8lb	11st 4lb	12st 2lb

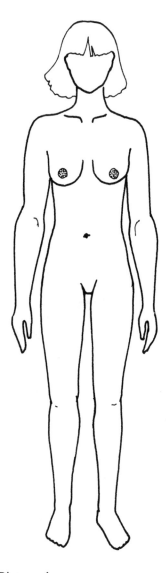
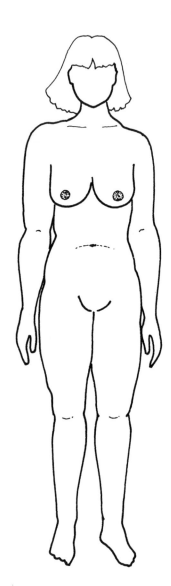

Diagram A

There are two other tests of proportion. Your thumb and first finger of either hand should meet around your wrist of the opposite hand; and if you hold your arms out level with your shoulders, the distance between your finger tips should equal your height. Do not be alarmed if you do not measure up to all these standards, however. They are just general indications, and the only thing that should give you concern is if you are overweight by more than just a few pounds.

During and after pregnancy, your figure will change. By the end of twenty weeks into pregnancy, your abdomen may be swollen and your navel protruding instead of being indented. Your breasts will enlarge. After you have had your baby, your abdominal organs may sag, and light exercises after a suitable period may be advisable to help tone up the abdominal muscles and restore your figure (see Chapter 20).

Before going further, however, you should learn to identify the muscles you wish to develop. Muscles are divided into three groups: voluntary, involuntary and cardiac. The voluntary ones are the only ones you can develop directly, because they are the only ones over which you have conscious control, but the others will benefit indirectly from your improved health and fitness.

Stand in front of a mirror, stripped, and with the aid of the following list and Diagrams B and C on pages 20 and 21, learn to pick out the different muscles. This is not a futile exercise. To develop a muscle, you must concentrate your attention on it, and you must know what movement it is designed to make.

Sterno mastoids The muscles at the sides of the neck. They turn the head from side to side, or lift it up and down.

Trapezius This muscle covers the shoulders and the upper part of the back of the neck. It turns the head and helps in any arm movement.

Deltoids The bands of muscle covering the shoulder joints. They raise the arms sideways or forwards.

Biceps The muscles at the front of the upper arm. They bend the arms.

Triceps The muscles at the back of the upper arm. They straighten the arm.

Pectorals The big triangular muscles at the front of the chest. They pull the arms in towards the body and help push away.

Serratus magnus The little ridges of muscle under the armpits. They lift the arms sideways.

Supinator longus The muscle at the side and back of the forearm. It turns the wrist from side to side.

Flexors (of the forearm) The muscles at the front of the forearm. They bend the wrist inwards.

External oblique abdominals These muscles extend down the sides of the body from the lower ribs. They turn the body and bend it from side to side.

Abdominals (upper and lower) These run from the lower ribs to the pubic bone at the front of the body. They bend the body forwards, and lift your legs in front of you.

Pectineus and adductor longus The muscles on the inside of the upper thigh which move the thigh inwards.

Rectus femoris The long muscle running down the front of the thigh. It raises the leg and straightens it.

Vastus internus The muscle at the side and back of the upper leg. It turns the leg.

Peroneus longus The muscle at the side of the lower leg. It helps turn the foot or rotate the leg.

Tibialis anticus The big muscle at the front of the calf. It bends the foot upwards.

Gastrocnemius and soleus These are at the side and back of the calf. The first bends the foot backwards; the main function of the second is to help you keep an upright posture.

Infra spinatus and rhomboideus major These muscles (Diagram C) are at the back of the shoulder. They take the shoulders back and help any pulling movement.

Latissimus dorsi The large muscles at the back of the upper body. They turn the body and help raise the arms.

Erector spinae The muscles in the small of the back. They straighten up the bent-over body.

Gluteus medius and gluteus maximus The fleshy muscles of the buttocks. They rotate and move the legs.

Vastus lateralis The muscle at the side and back of the upper leg. It bends the knee and raises the leg sideways.

Adductor magnus The muscle at the back of the inside of the upper leg. It turns the leg as when pointing the foot outwards.

Biceps of the leg and semi-tendinosus These two muscles are at the back of the upper leg. They bend the leg backwards.

Tensor muscles and vastus externus The tensor muscle covers the hip; the vastus externus runs from it down the outside of the thigh. They lift the leg sideways.

These are not all the muscles you have, of course – as already stated, there are over 600 – but these are the ones that will concern you as a weight trainer.

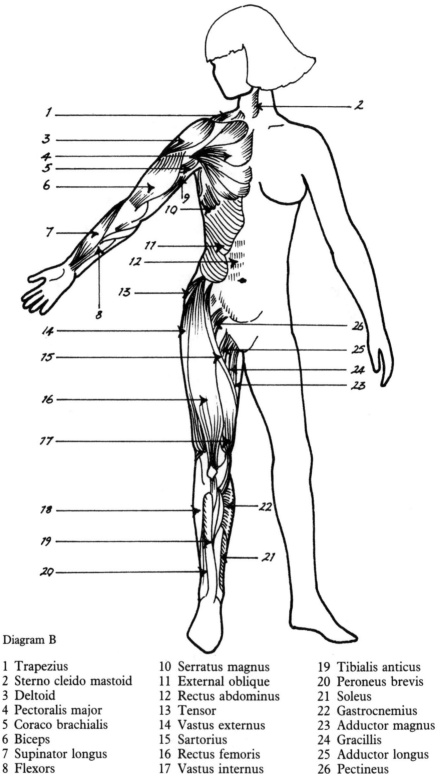

Diagram B

1 Trapezius	10 Serratus magnus	19 Tibialis anticus
2 Sterno cleido mastoid	11 External oblique	20 Peroneus brevis
3 Deltoid	12 Rectus abdominus	21 Soleus
4 Pectoralis major	13 Tensor	22 Gastrocnemius
5 Coraco brachialis	14 Vastus externus	23 Adductor magnus
6 Biceps	15 Sartorius	24 Gracillis
7 Supinator longus	16 Rectus femoris	25 Adductor longus
8 Flexors	17 Vastus internus	26 Pectineus
9 Triceps	18 Peroneus longus	

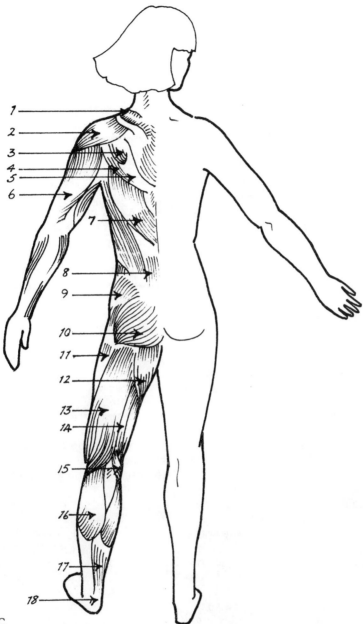

Diagram C

1 Trapezius	10 Gluteus maximus
2 Deltoid	11 Vastus lateralis
3 Infra spinatus	12 Adductor magnus
4 Teres major	13 Biceps
5 Rhomboideus major	14 Semi-tendinosus
6 Triceps	15 Semi-membranosus
7 Latissimus dorsi	16 Gastrocnemius
8 Erector spinae	17 Soleus
9 Gluteus medius	18 Tendo achillus

4 Eating for Health

To maintain normal good health, the body needs adequate supplies of protein, fats, carbohydrates, dietary fibre, vitamins and minerals. Let us look at each in turn.

Protein People of all ages need protein. Our flesh is protein; therefore, to renew cells, heal wounds and build muscle we need a regular supply. Proteins are made up of small amino acids which are found in all animal foods: meat, poultry, fish, eggs, milk, cheese and yoghurt. Low-value proteins are also found in soya, wheat, potatoes, nuts and pulse vegetables.

Fats Fats have an important dietary role apart from the main one of supplying energy. They make food palatable in taste and smell; they literally 'oil' the digestive system; they are needed in absorbing certain vitamins. All these functions can be achieved with very small amounts of fat. The main sources are: hard margarines, milk, cheese and meat for the saturated fats; soft margarines, cereals, nuts, fish and poultry for the polyunsaturated fats.

Carbohydrates All starches and sugars are carbohydrates and these are converted into glucose and other simple sugars, which are used for energy or stored as fat in the body. Most carbohydrate foods contain other nutrients, except sugar which is purely carbohydrate. The main sources are: bread, flour, cereals, sugar and potatoes. Alcohol is used by the body as a carbohydrate.

Dietary fibre Dietary fibre comes mainly from plant cell walls, and is carbohydrate in nutrient value. There are two types of fibre: insoluble fibre which is found mainly in wheat products, flour, bread, breakfast cereals, bran and the more fibrous vegetables, and soluble fibre which is contained in all fruit and vegetables, though the richest sources are pulses, red kidney beans, baked beans, dried peas, lentils, oats and barley products. Fibre is an important part of our daily diet for several reasons: it stimulates the digestive system; it prevents constipation; it reduces the absorption of fat and sugar; it makes us feel 'full' and so reduces our appetite when we want to slim.

Vitamins Without vitamins the body cannot make full use of the other nutrients for energy, growth and repair of body tissue. If you have a good varied diet, you will get all the vitamins you need.

Vitamin A is found in liver, cheese, milk, eggs, butter, margarine, fish liver oils, spinach, carrots and apricots. Vitamin A helps us fight infection by strengthening the cell walls to prevent viruses and bacteria from entering. It is also good for the skin and the eyesight.

Group B vitamins are found in meat, especially liver and pork, flour, bread, eggs, cheese, milk and yeast. Folic acid, a B vitamin necessary for the formation of DNA and cell nuclei, is in offal and raw green vegetables. B vitamins help to break down carbohydrates, proteins and fats, and to release energy, and they are essential for the functioning of our nervous system. As B vitamins cannot be stored in our bodies, we need a daily supply.

Vitamin C is found in green vegetables, fresh fruit, especially citrus fruits and blackcurrants, and potatoes. Vitamin C helps us to fight infections and keeps our skin healthy. It also helps us to absorb iron. This vitamin cannot be stored in the body and must be included in our daily diet.

Vitamin D is found in fish liver oils, fatty fish, margarine, eggs and butter, and is also produced in the body by the action of the sun on our skin. It is needed to help us absorb and use the minerals calcium and phosphorus, which build strong bones and healthy teeth.

Vitamin E is found in most vegetable oils, cereal products and eggs. It helps in the body's use of oxygen, and is therefore valuable to anyone doing vigorous exercise.

Minerals A well-balanced diet should contain small amounts of different minerals, particularly calcium and iron. Calcium is vital as this forms the structure of our teeth and bones, and is in constant demand. It is found in dark green vegetables, milk, cheese, fish and beans. Iron is needed for the formation of red blood cells which carry oxygen around the body. Oxygen is needed to produce energy and is thus essential for the proper functioning of our body. Due to hormonal development, menstruation and menopause, women need more iron than men. Good sources are liver, kidneys, fish, wholemeal bread, eggs, green vegetables, peas, beans, dried fruit and breakfast cereals. Salt is important to maintain the correct fluid balance and blood pressure; too much salt can cause high blood pressure.

Water Water is essential to life, so obviously it must be included in a well-balanced diet. At least 8 to 9 cups of liquid are considered necessary every day.

Because our bodies need a constant fresh supply of certain minerals and vitamins, the best way to make sure of getting them is to follow a three-meal-a-day weekly plan, which allows you to digest and absorb the nutrients at regular intervals. Do not allow too long a gap between meals. Four to five hours is the recommended time.

Pages 24 and 25 give a nutritionally balanced Seven-day Meal Plan suitable for a woman of medium size leading a moderately active life. It is based on 2,000 calories per day. Put it on the wall in your kitchen, and follow it, and you will not have to think what the next meal is going to be.

If you plan your week's meals along the lines suggested, you will soon feel fitter and look trimmer, and you will have more energy because your body will be getting all the nutrients it needs. Note that all the weights quoted for meat and fish are the cooked weights.

A few other points:

Use 1pt/600ml skimmed milk, or ½pt/300ml full cream milk every day, and up to 5fl oz/150ml yoghurt, if desired as well. This milk allowance includes that used in drinks and in cooking.

Try to cut down sugar to a minimum. Remember 1oz/30g will add 112 calories to your diet. If alcohol is drunk, this too will add calories. 10fl oz/300ml beer is approximately 90 calories, and a glass of wine is 80 calories.

Tea or coffee may be drunk as desired.

If you wish, you may add to the above menus 1 sweet biscuit, or 1 cake, or 1 bun, or 2oz/60g of sweets or chocolate each day.

Eat at least one serving of green vegetables every day. Remember that fresh raw fruit and vegetables provide more vitamins than the same quantities when cooked.

Seven-day meal plan for health

DAY 1

Breakfast
1 orange
1 boiled egg
1 slice wholemeal bread
2tsp margarine or butter

Lunch
4oz/120g tuna fish
1 bread roll
2tsp margarine
Salad of lettuce, tomato, onion, cucumber and
  beetroot
2tsp vegetable oil
1 apple

Supper
4oz/120g chicken, cooked in a casserole with
  8oz/240g mixed vegetables consisting of carrots, onions, parsnips and swede
6oz/180g potato
4oz/120g green vegetables
1 pear topped with 1tbsp chocolate sauce

* * *

DAY 2

Breakfast
½ grapefruit
1oz/30g bran cereal with
2½fl.oz/75ml yoghurt
1 slice wholemeal bread
2tsp margarine
2tsp marmalade

Lunch
4oz/120g cooked ham
6oz/180g mixed bean salad, with red, haricot and
  chick beans combined with 2tsp oil, chopped
  parsley and chopped onion
Lettuce
Tomato
1 slice melon

Supper
10fl oz/300ml vegetable soup made from 1 stock
  cube and mixed vegetables
6oz/180g fish in breadcrumbs
4oz/120g potato
4oz/120g carrots
4oz/120g green vegetables
4fl oz/120ml parsley sauce
Baked apple stuffed with 1oz/30g dried fruit and
  topped with 2tsp honey

* * *

DAY 3

Breakfast
4fl oz/120ml unsweetened orange juice
3oz/90g sardines
1 slice bread
2tsp margarine
1 tomato

Lunch
10fl oz/300ml tomato soup
4oz/120g cottage cheese, topped with 1oz/30g
  grated hard cheese
4 crispbreads
2tsp margarine
Salad or cooked vegetables including green
  vegetables, celery, onion, carrots
1 peach

Supper
3oz/90g sautéd onions
4oz/120g liver
4oz/120g spinach
2 tomatoes
4oz/120g cooked brown rice
6oz/180g fresh fruit salad
2½fl oz/75ml yoghurt

* * *

DAY 4

Breakfast
5oz/150g grapes
1 scrambled egg
1 tomato
1 slice wholemeal bread
2tsp margarine

Lunch
Macaroni cheese using 4oz/120g cooked macaroni, 3oz/90g grated cheese, 4oz/120g cooked
  mushrooms
4oz/120g cooked cauliflower with 5fl oz/150g
  white sauce topped with 2tsp toasted sesame
  seeds
4oz/120g green beans
1 orange

If you work away from home and find this
unsuitable to carry, substitute:
3oz/90g cheese
2oz/60g bread roll with sesame seeds
2tsp margarine
mixed salad
1 orange

Supper
6oz/180g mackerel (canned or fresh)
4oz/120g sauté potatoes
4oz/120g peas
large green salad
6oz/180g stewed fruit
2½ fl oz/75ml yoghurt

★ ★ ★

DAY 5

Breakfast
1 banana
1½oz/45g muesli
5fl oz/150ml yoghurt
1 slice wholemeal bread
2tsp margarine
1tsp marmite
1 tomato

Lunch
1oz/30g bread
4oz/120g baked beans
1 egg
1oz/30g grated cheese
Large mixed salad
2tsp mayonnaise
6oz/180g pineapple

As an alternative, have:
1 small bread roll
Cold baked beans
Boiled egg
1oz/30g cheese
1 apple

Supper
6oz/180g salmon (fresh or tinned)
Cucumber
4oz/120g corn on the cob
2oz/60g green beans
Sliced green pepper
4 crispbreads
2tsp margarine
1 orange set in 5fl oz/150ml jelly

★ ★ ★

DAY 6

Breakfast
½ grapefruit
1 slice bacon
1 egg

1 tomato
1 slice wholemeal bread
2tsp margarine

Lunch
6oz/180g jacket potato or a bread roll filled with
    4oz/120g cooked shrimps, and garnished with
    chopped parsley
Lettuce
Cucumber
Tomato
Grated carrot
Chopped celery
2tsp vegetable oil
1 pear

Supper
4oz/120g turkey
1oz/30g herb stuffing
4oz/120g pasta cooked and mixed with 3oz/90g
    cooked peas and 3oz/90g green pepper
4oz/120g spinach
5oz/150g blackcurrants
2½fl oz/75ml yoghurt

★ ★ ★

DAY 7

Breakfast
4oz/120g pineapple
1½oz/45g porridge, uncooked weight
5fl oz/150ml milk
2tsp honey
1 slice wholemeal bread
2tsp margarine

Lunch
4oz/120g beef
3oz/90g Yorkshire pudding
4oz/120g baked jacket potato
4oz/120g spring greens
4oz/120g carrots
2fl oz/60ml gravy
1 slice apple pie
5fl oz/150ml custard

Supper
4oz/120g canned drained pilchards
Mixed salad of lettuce, tomato, cucumber, and
    spring onions
2tsp mayonnaise
2 crispbreads
2 plums

25

5 Eating to Slim

To slim, we not only have to exercise, but we also have to reduce our food intake, so that the energy used up by our bodies is greater than that created by the food we eat. In this way, we use up our store of extra fat.

It is important, therefore, to know what foods we really need to eat, and how we can cut down on the non-essential extras. Read the information on nutrients and where they are found given in the preceding chapter, so that you will fully understand how important the correct diet is for general fitness and well-being. Then decide how much weight you want to lose by consulting the tables on page 17, and plan a target date on which to reach that weight. Make up your mind that nothing and no one are going to deter you, and that you will exercise and diet sensibly until you do succeed. A healthy weight loss to expect would average out at 2lb per week.

As the energy value of food and drink is measured in calories, and many foods are now labelled with their calorific value, it is important to understand what this actually means in terms of the food you are going to eat. The recognised measurement of energy is as follows:

1oz/30g of carbohydrate provides nearly 110 calories.
1oz/30g of fat provides nearly 260 calories.
1oz/30g of protein provides just over 110 calories.
1fl oz/30ml of alcohol provides nearly 200 calories.

Most foods contain a mixture of nutrients, with the other components of minerals, vitamins and water providing no calories, so the calorie value of any food is calculated by the carbohydrate, fat, protein and alcohol content.

A calorie guide is worth using, and is a great deterrent when tempted to snack on say a handful of nuts, a packet of crisps or a bar of chocolate. You can see in your guide how each one of these would add almost 200 calories to your intake and the snack would be gone in a flash. Those calories could have been used on foods that would have satisfied your appetite longer and which would have had better nutritional value. Hence the Seven-day Slimmers' Meal Plan is recommended because it has an in-built discipline and gives you the confidence of knowing that the lower-calorie meals are still providing all your required nutrients. It should give you a feeling of satisfaction as well.

How can we economise on calories? Let us consider the various foods.

Meat Always remove all fat and skin. Remember that chicken and turkey are lower in fat than beef, lamb, pork, goose and duck. Liver, kidney and heart contain very little fat. Sausages, beefburgers and faggots contain higher proportions of fat and carbohydrates than lean meat. Salami, garlic sausage, pâtés and luncheon meats are all higher in fat content than cold meats. When using minced meat, start by frying it gently to remove all the fat.

Fish Eat white fish, such as cod, hake, plaice and haddock, rather than oily fish such as herrings, kippers and mackerel. Do not use the batter-coated frozen fish, which needs frying. With canned fish, such as tuna or sardines, choose the kind tinned in brine rather than oil, but if you do use the oily ones, drain off all the oil. Shellfish is low in calories.

Eggs Most of the fat in eggs is in the yolk, therefore the yolk contains most of the calories, not the white.

Milk Considered a complete food, milk should therefore be included in your diet. Use skimmed milk, either liquid or powdered. Cream is very high in fat, and should not be taken when slimming. Natural yoghurt is a good alternative to cream; a small carton contains about 75 calories, but the sweetened fruit yoghurts can contain up to 175 calories.

Fats All fats are very high in calories, so only a small amount is needed each day. Low-fat spreads contain half the calories of margarine. Grilling food instead of frying removes extra fat.

Cheese Hard cheeses are high in fat and therefore in calories, and must be eaten sparingly. Low-fat cheeses such as cottage and curd cheese are a useful source of protein.

Vegetables They contain a high percentage of water but also supply considerable quantities of nutrients, so are therefore extremely important in your slimming plan. Green leaf vegetables have no calories; root vegetables have very few. Because vegetables are bulky and slow down our eating, they make us feel full. Frying vegetables multiplies their calorie count three or four times, so boil, bake, steam or purée vegetables, and eat the skin or rind whenever possible. Beans, peas and sweetcorn have a particularly high fibre content.

Fruit The sweeter the fruit, the more calories it contains. If sugar is used to sweeten stewed fruit the calories are greatly increased, so use a low-calorie sweetener instead.

Bread Eat a variety of breads. Wholemeal and bran-enriched breads provide extra fibre in the diet. Low-calorie breads contain more air, so they contain fewer calories slice for slice.

Breakfast cereals The unsweetened lightweight cereals and porridge are lowest in calories. If you must sweeten them use a sugar substitute, and always count any milk or yoghurt that you add as part of your daily allowance.

Rice and pasta These are very useful additions to our diet, but fried rice would greatly increase the calorific value. Brown rice and wholemeal pasta are good sources of fibre.

Biscuits and cakes These are best forgotten when trying to lose weight. If you really cannot do without, eat the small plain wholemeal biscuits.

Sugar Sugar is not needed nutritionally and is better cut out altogether. Use a sugar substitute if you need.

Alcohol Alcoholic drinks, too, are better left out when slimming, as they provide no appreciable nutrient value. Choose low-calorie soft drinks or mineral water instead.

Make sure that you include in your slimming diet the following items every day:
1pt/600ml skimmed milk, liquid or powdered, or ½pt/300ml skimmed milk and 5fl oz/150ml natural yoghurt.
3 fruits.
At least 1 green vegetable, as well as salad and cooked vegetables.
Meat, fish, poultry, eggs, cheese or pulses in at least two meals.
Bread, cereals, potatoes or pasta.
Small quantities of fat to be taken with your meals, eg margarine, oil or salad cream.

The plan on pages 28 and 29 is based on 1,200 calories per day. Put it up on your kitchen wall, and follow it. If you have to take these meals to the office, many of them can be put up in plastic containers or screw-top jars.

In following the plan, weigh portions carefully. Note that spoon measurements mean level spoonfuls, not heaped. Where 2tsp of low-fat spread are listed, you may change this to 1tsp of polyunsaturated margarine, if you prefer. You may substitute skimmed milk for yoghurt if you wish. Herbs and spices improve the flavour of the recipes tremendously and, as they contain no calories, can be widely used.

You may interchange the lunch and supper meals, but try to have the three meals listed all in the same day, as the calories on each day add up to approximately 1,200.

Using this meal plan and exercising as recommended in Chapter 15, you will lose your extra weight and flabbiness, and when you reach your goal weight you will look firm and trim as well as slim.

Seven-day Slimmers' Meal Plan

DAY 1

Breakfast
1 orange
1 boiled egg
1oz/30g wholemeal bread
2tsp low-fat spread

Lunch
3oz/90g tuna fish
Salad of lettuce, onion rings and
    1 tomato
2 celery sticks
1oz/30g beetroot
2tsp salad cream
2 crispbreads (50 calories)
1 apple

Supper
3oz/90g chicken without skin cooked in casserole
    with
3oz/90g carrots
4oz/120g onions
2oz/60g parsnips
3oz/90g turnips
3oz/90g jacket potato
4oz/120g cooked green vegetable
1 pear

★　★　★

DAY 2

Breakfast
½ grapefruit
1oz/30g bran cereal
2½fl oz/75ml natural yoghurt

Lunch
3oz/90g lean ham
3oz/90g mixed bean salad, using red, haricot,
    chick etc
1tsp chopped parsley
2oz/60g chopped onions
Salad of lettuce, 1 tomato, cucumber and celery
2tsp vegetable oil
1 medium slice melon

Supper
Vegetable soup using 1 stock cube, and 6oz/180g
    celery, onion and carrot
4oz/120g white fish cooked in 4fl oz/120g skim-
    med milk, thickened with 1tsp cornflour and
    chopped parsley
4oz/120g green beans
1tsp margarine
1 baked apple cooked in 2tbsp low-calorie lemon
    drink

★　★　★

DAY 3

Breakfast
4oz/120ml unsweetened orange or grapefruit
    juice
2oz/60g drained sardines
1oz/30g bread
2tsp low-fat spread
1 tomato

Lunch
4oz/120g cottage cheese
2 crispbreads (50 calories)
Salad of 1 tomato, celery, cucumber, grated
    carrot, shredded cabbage, onion and red
    pepper
2tsp low-fat spread
1 banana (medium sized)

Supper
3oz/90g sautéd onion in 2tsp vegetable oil. Add
    3oz/90g liver and sauté (7 minutes' cooking
    time).
3oz/90g cooked brown rice
4oz/120g spinach
1 tomato
4oz/120g mushrooms
4oz/120g fresh fruit salad
2½oz/75ml natural yoghurt

★　★　★

DAY 4

Breakfast
4oz/120g grapes
1 scrambled egg
1 tomato
1oz/30g bread
2tsp low-fat spread

Lunch
Macaroni cheese made with
3oz/90g cooked macaroni
2oz/60g grated cheese mixed with 3oz/90g
    mushrooms and 3oz/90g cauliflower (cooked
    weights) blended with 2fl oz/50ml skimmed
    milk. Sprinkle the top with 1tsp toasted
    sesame seeds. Serve with mixed salad of let-
    tuce, tomato, celery and chives.
1 orange

A suitable alternative if you have to take lunch to
the office would be:
2oz/60g cheese
2oz/60g bread roll
Mixed salad
2tsp mayonnaise
1 orange

Supper
4oz/120g mackerel, canned or fresh
3oz/90g potato
3oz/90g peas
3oz/90g carrots
1 apple

⋆ ⋆ ⋆

DAY 5

Breakfast
3oz/90g stewed prunes with their juice
1½oz/45g muesli
5fl oz/150ml natural yoghurt

Lunch
3oz/90g baked beans
1 egg
1oz/30g bread
2tsp low-fat spread
Mixed salad of grated cabbage, onion, carrot,
    celery and peppers
4oz/120g pineapple

An alternative for the office would be:
Cold baked beans
1 boiled egg
1oz/30g bread
2tsp low-fat spread
Mixed salad
1 apple

Supper
4oz/120g salmon, fresh or canned
Cucumber
2oz/60g corn on the cob
2oz/60g green beans
2oz/60g pepper
2tsp low-fat spread
1 orange

⋆ ⋆ ⋆

DAY 6

Breakfast
½ grapefruit
1 poached egg
1 tomato
3oz/90g mushrooms
2tsp low-fat spread

Lunch
3oz/90g jacket potato with centre scooped out
    and filled with 3oz/90g shrimps
Chopped parsley
2tsp salad cream
Large mixed salad of lettuce, celery, cucumber,
    pepper and spring onion
1 pear

If packing a lunch for the office, replace the
jacket potato with a 2oz/60g bread roll.

Supper
4oz/120g cooked turkey, no skin
3oz/90g cooked pasta mixed with
2oz/60g cooked peas
2oz/60g cooked celery
1tbsp chopped chives or spring onions
1tsp vegetable oil and
4oz/120g spinach
5oz/150g blackcurrants
2½fl oz/75ml natural yoghurt

⋆ ⋆ ⋆

DAY 7

Breakfast
4oz/120g pineapple
1oz/30g porridge (uncooked weight)
5fl oz/150ml skimmed milk
2tsp honey

Lunch
3oz/90g lean beef
3oz/90g baked jacket potato
2tsp low-fat spread
4oz/120g spring greens
3oz/90g carrots
3oz/90g boiled parsnips
5oz/150g strawberries
2½fl oz/75ml natural yoghurt

A suitable alternative for the office would be:
3oz/90g lean beef
2oz/60g bread
2tsp low-fat spread
Mixed salad
1 apple

Supper
3oz/90g canned drained pilchards
Mixed salad of lettuce, tomato, celery, cucumber
    and peppers
3 crispbreads
2tsp low-fat spread
4oz/120g plums

When you have reached your correct
weight, start adding an additional 50 calories per day on to this Slimmers' Meal Plan,
so that you gradually move back up to the
normal 2,000 calories per day of the Plan
For Health (Chapter 4), but watch your
weight, and if it starts creeping up again,
stop adding calories. Once your weight is
stable, you have reached the calorie level
your body needs to cope with your current
level of activity.

6 Eating to Develop

When building muscle, more protein is needed. Diet has to be adjusted in much the same way as someone taking up heavy manual work would have to eat more than when she was following a sedentary occupation. This means increasing calorie intake each day, so that more energy is taken in in food than is used up in output. The extra calories build you up. It is essential to plan these extra calories wisely by choosing nutritious high-protein high-carbohydrate foods, so that you develop firm muscles and a shapely body.

An American body-building champion was once a very thin model who decided to reshape her body. After four years of hard training and eating 5,000 to 8,000 calories per day, she succeeded in building her physique to championship standard. Before a contest, she then had to diet rigorously on 700 calories per day to disperse the layer of fat under the skin, so that she could define her flexed muscles in the poses required for the contest. Americans use terms like 'pumping lace' and 'being ripped' for these preparations. Of course, this champion was training at a more advanced level than most women will want to do, but her experience does demonstrate how essential it is to combine correct diet with exercises to build the shape you desire.

Look at the height and weight table in Chapter 3 and decide how much weight you want to put on, and consider how you will achieve the increase. Either you can increase your proteins and carbohydrates at normal meal times, or you can have snacks between meals to absorb the extra needed. If you break up your meals into six smaller ones in this way you will not feel so full, and your digestive system will have a better chance of using the food to the full for building your physique. Suggested meal times could be: Breakfast 7.30am, snack 10am, lunch 1pm, snack 5pm, dinner 8pm, snack 10pm.

Foods To Avoid
When planning your increase, avoid greasy foods, high-fat and high-sugar foods, sweets, sugar, soft drinks, alcoholic beverages, syrups, jams, jellies, white flour, white bread. These will take the edge off your appetite for the more nutritious foods you should be eating.

Foods To Add
Eat more meat such as pork, beef, lamb, seafood, potatoes, fruit, vegetables, nuts, peanut butter, beans, corn, rice, coconut, wholemeal flour products such as cereals, bread, biscuits and noodles, whole-milk products, ice cream, cream cheese, yoghurt, dates, figs and raisins.

If you decide that you are still only going to have three meals per day, adding the additional protein and carbohydrate requisites to the Meal Plan For Health in Chapter 4, you must aim to add 1,000 calories every day choosing from the list of 'Foods to Add' above. The calorie chart includes most of the foods discussed in these three chapters.

Calorie chart

Meat	Weight	Calories
Bacon, 1 grilled back rasher	1oz/30g	80
Beef, sirloin roast	1oz/30g	50
Beefburger, large grilled	4oz/120g	240
Corned beef	1oz/30g	60
Ham, boiled lean	1oz/30g	47
Lamb, leg roast	1oz/30g	54
Liver pâté	1oz/30g	90
Pork, joint roast	1oz/30g	56
Salami	1oz/30g	130
Sausage, beef, large grilled	–	130

Poultry, game, offal		
Chicken, roast, meat only	1oz/30g	42
Duck, meat only, roast	1oz/30g	54
Heart, roast, ox	1oz/30g	50
Kidney, lamb's fried	1oz/30g	65
Liver, lamb's fried	1oz/30g	66
Rabbit, stewed	1oz/30g	51
Turkey, roast	1oz/30g	40

Fish		
Cod, baked or grilled	1oz/30g	27
Crab, canned	1oz/30g	25
Haddock, fillet fried in breadcrumbs	1oz/30g	50
Herring, grilled on the bone	1oz/30g	38
Kipper, fillet grilled or baked	1oz/30g	58
Mackerel	1oz/30g	53
Pilchards, canned in tomato sauce	1oz/30g	36
Prawns, boiled shelled	1oz/30g	30
Salmon, steamed or poached	1oz/30g	56
Sardines, canned in tomato sauce	1oz/30g	50
Shrimps	1oz/30g	33
Trout, grilled or poached on the bone	1oz/30g	25
Tuna, drained of oil	1oz/30g	60
Fish fingers, grilled, 2	–	100

Eggs		
Egg, size 3, boiled or poached	–	80
Egg, fried	–	100
Omelette, 2 eggs	–	160

Green and salad vegetables		
Beans, runner, boiled	1oz/30g	5
Beetroot	1oz/30g	12
Brussels sprouts, boiled	1oz/30g	5
Cabbage	1oz/30g	4
Carrots, raw	1oz/30g	6
Cauliflower	1oz/30g	3
Celery, raw	1oz/30g	2
Cucumber	1oz/30g	3
Lettuce, raw	1oz/30g	3
Mushrooms, raw	1oz/30g	4
Onions, raw	1oz/30g	7
Peas, boiled	1oz/30g	15
Peppers, raw	1oz/30g	4
Spinach	1oz/30g	9
Spring greens, boiled	1oz/30g	4
Tomatoes, raw	1oz/30g	4

Low-calorie drinks		
Bovril, 1 tsp	–	10
Coffee, no milk or sugar	–	–
Orange juice, unsweetened	5fl oz/150 ml	50
Oxo cube, meat	–	15
Tea, no milk or sugar	–	–
Tomato juice	5fl oz/150 ml	20
Water	–	–

Fruit		
Apple, raw	1oz/30g	10
Apricot, fresh with stone	1oz/30g	7
Banana, flesh only	1oz/30g	22
Blackberries, raw	1oz/30g	8
Blackcurrants	1oz/30g	8
Cherries, fresh with stone	1oz/30g	12
Dates, dried without stones	1oz/30g	70
Gooseberries, ripe dessert	1oz/30g	10
Grapes, white	1oz/30g	17
Lemon, whole	–	15
Melon, with skin	1oz/30g	4
Orange, large	–	75
Peach, fresh with stone	1oz/30g	9
Pear, whole	1oz/30g	8
Pineapple, fresh, flesh only	1oz/30g	13
Prunes, stewed with stones, no sugar	1oz/30g	21
Raisins, sultanas, currants	1oz/30g	70
Raspberries, fresh	1oz/30g	7
Rhubarb, uncooked weight	1oz/30g	2
Strawberries, fresh	1oz/30g	7

Cereals		
Bran-enriched cereals	1oz/30g	80

Cornflakes	1oz/30g	100
Muesli	1oz/30g	110
Porridge	1oz/30g	105

Milk

Milk, whole	1fl oz/30ml	20
Milk, skimmed	1fl oz/30ml	10
Custard	¼ pt/120ml	175
Ice cream	1fl oz/30ml	50
Rice pudding	6oz/180g	160
Yoghurt, fruit	5floz/150 ml	175
Yoghurt, low fat	1oz/30g	15
Yoghurt, whole milk	1oz/30g	25

Cheese

Brie	1oz/30g	88
Cheddar	1oz/30g	120
Cottage	1oz/30g	27
Cream	1oz/30g	125
Curd	1oz/30g	54
Edam	1oz/30g	90
Stilton	1oz/30g	131

Bread

Bread, white	1oz/30g	66
Crispbread	1 slice	30
Wheatgerm	1oz/30g	65
Wholemeal	1oz/30g	61

Rice and pasta

Macaroni	1oz/30g	33
Pasta, wholewheat boiled	1oz/30g	34
Rice, brown boiled	1oz/30g	33

Root vegetables and pulses

Baked beans in tomato sauce	1oz/30g	20
Butter beans, boiled	1oz/30g	27
Kidney beans, red boiled	1oz/30g	25
Carrots, raw	1oz/30g	6
Leeks, raw weight	1oz/30g	9
Lentils, raw weight	1oz/30g	86
Lentils, boiled weight	1oz/30g	28
Onions, raw	1oz/30g	7
Parsnips, raw	1oz/30g	14
Potatoes, baked with skins	1oz/30g	24
Swedes	1oz/30g	6
Sweetcorn, canned in brine	1oz/30g	22
Sweetcorn, whole medium cob	–	155
Turnips	1oz/30g	6

Fats

Butter	1oz/30g	210
Lard	1oz/30g	253
Margarine, low-fat spread	1oz/30g	105
Margarine	1oz/30g	210

Mayonnaise	1fl oz/30g	205
Oil, sunflower	1fl oz/30g	255
Peanut butter	1oz/30g	177
Salad cream, low calorie	½fl oz/15ml	45

Biscuits, cakes, pastry

Biscuits, plain digestive	–	70
Chocolate biscuit	–	130
Semi-sweet rich tea biscuit	–	50
Cake, plain fruit	4oz/120g	360
Cake, sponge	3oz/90g	400
Currant bun	–	250
Danish pastry	1	239
Date and nut bread	1 slice	215
Doughnut with jam	2oz/60g	200
Oat cakes	1	45
Pastry, flaky	1oz/30g	160
Pastry, short	1oz/30g	150
Pie, apple	6oz/180g	300
Pie, steak and kidney	8oz/240g	735
Sausage roll, flaky pastry	2oz/60g	270
Scone	1oz/30g	100
Yorkshire pudding	1oz/30g	60

Sugar, sweets, chocolate, preserves

Chocolate	1oz/30g	130
Golden syrup	1oz/30g	84
Honey	1oz/30g	82
Jam or marmalade	1oz/30g	74
Sugar	1oz/30g	112
Sweets, boiled	1oz/30g	105
Toffees	1oz/30g	130

Cream

Clotted	1fl oz/30ml	165
Double	1fl oz/30ml	127
Single	1fl oz/30ml	60

Crisps and nuts

Crisps, potato	1oz/30g	150
Peanuts, roasted	1oz/30g	162
Sesame seeds	1 tbsp	55
Tofu (soya bean curd)	1oz/30g	16

Alcoholic Drinks

Beer	½ pt	85
Cider	½ pt	100
Spirits – brandy, gin, rum, vodka, whisky	25ml	50
Wine, dry	4fl oz	75
Wine, sweet	4fl oz	105

With the above chart you can make your own Seven-day Meal Plan. By comparing the calorific value of food in the same food groups you will soon learn what you need and how much.

If, instead of adding quantities to the Meal Plan for Health, you choose to introduce snacks as a way of increasing your calories, the following Suggested Snacks for One Week could be inserted into the Meal Plan for Health, eating them at the times between meals suggested earlier. These take your calorie count up to 3,000 per day.

Suggested Snacks for One Week

DAY 1

Morning
1 sausage roll

Afternoon
Peanut butter sandwich using 2 slices wholemeal bread

Evening
2oz/60g cereal with 10fl oz/300ml milk

* * *

DAY 2

Morning
4oz/120g peanuts and raisins

Afternoon
2oz/60g ice cream with 2 shortbread biscuits

Evening
1 slice fruit pie with 5fl oz/150ml milk

* * *

DAY 3

Morning
2oz/60g cheese sandwiched between 2 slices wholemeal or granary bread

Afternoon
1 banana with 1 scone and 2tsp margarine

Evening
6oz/180g rice pudding with 1 sliced pear

* * *

DAY 4

Morning
3oz/90g liver pâté with 2 crispbreads and 2tsp margarine

Afternoon
1 bun with 2 tsp margarine and 1 egg

Evening
2 chocolate biscuits with 5fl oz/150ml milk

* * *

DAY 5

Morning
2 slices date and nut bread

Afternoon
3oz/90g sardines on toast with 2tsp margarine

Evening
5fl oz/150ml fruit yoghurt with 2 sweet biscuits

* * *

DAY 6

Morning
1 Danish pastry

Afternoon
3oz/90g corned beef in sandwich made with 2 slices wholemeal bread and 2tsp margarine

Evening
2 digestive biscuits with 5fl oz/150ml milk

* * *

DAY 7

Morning
2 oatcakes with 3oz/90g cream cheese

Afternoon
1 slice fruit cake

Evening
4oz/120g baked beans on toast

Follow all the instructions given with the Meal Plan For Health in Chapter 4, preferably using whole milk. You may interchange the snacks if you wish, but aim to add 1,000 calories per day.

The great benefit of planning meals ahead is that you need not worry about 'Food' every day. 'What am I going to eat?' 'Will it make me fat?' 'Will I lose too much weight?' 'Am I eating the right foods for my health?'. With these three balanced diets, one-week-at-a-time meal plans, you can relax your attitude to food and enjoy eating much more because you know what you are getting is right for you.

Soon you will see the benefits in clear skin, and hair, teeth, nails and eyes in peak condition, and you will experience a general feeling of well-being. Remember, always, fitness depends on exercise and on a healthy and varied diet.

7 The Psychology of Training

How are you going to fit all this in to your normal busy life, you may ask. This is where the psychological approach will come to your aid. You must want to train; you must keep your motivation before you; you must use every trick to encourage you to persevere; you must reward your efforts. Training is a serious business. Only by a permanent commitment to planned eating and regular exercise can you hope to achieve lasting and worthwhile results.

Consider first the very real benefits that are offered to you. Health is the first, and it is a priceless gift. Our grandparents and great-grandparents would consider that we were very inactive today, with all our modern conveniences of washing machines, vacuum cleaners, central heating, etc, and activity is essential for health. You grow old and weak because you stop exercising, not the other way round. So, finding the exercise to suit you is of paramount importance.

Most women who have recognised the need for exercise have chosen to take up sports they enjoy, such as swimming, jogging, dancing, and more recently they have discovered that weight training gets results in a shorter time than other sports. A shapely figure is another of the benefits that women seek. Here weight training brings amazing results, especially if combined with dieting. Firm rounded arms and shoulders, neat bust, tight bottom and shapely legs are no longer a dream. They are a possibility.

One lady found that she was able to firm up her bust sensationally after breast-feeding. Another with flabby upper legs was able to lose 23in around each thigh. Weight training will whip you into shape in a few weeks, toning and firming your muscles, making you look and feel better than ever

before, and above all making you fitter to face life's problems. Do not be afraid that it will make you look muscular or masculine; it will make you more shapely and feminine, if done correctly. Many glamorous television and stage stars now train with weights.

A good feeling is another of the benefits. There is nothing quite like the inner glow of fitness and the satisfaction that comes of knowing you have done your best for your body. Pre-menstrual tension and feelings of frustration and irritability are greatly alleviated by a general work-out. The flow of blood into all parts of the body is stimulated and everything functions better.

First, make up your mind why you want to train. Is it for health, for a better figure, to improve your performance at some sport? Having decided this, start out with confidence. It is said that weight training is one sport where there are no losers, because as soon as you pick up a barbell or dumb-bell you are making that tiny bit of improvement. Unlike other sports, you are not competing against anyone, only yourself.

Then, keep your motivation before you. Think how good you will look on the beach next summer, or how much more attractive you will be to your boyfriend or husband, or how pleased your athletics coach will be when you win the mile. This visualisation of the end helps to maintain enthusiasm, and two of the enemies of success are boredom and lack of perseverance – they often go hand in hand. When you consider how much training is required for some of the more spectacular results and how much discipline is needed to keep it up on a regular basis, you may feel weight training is not for you. Do not give in. Everyone feels like that sometimes, and there are tricks that will help you keep going.

First, choose whether you are going to be happier training at home or in a gym. It will depend on your personality. Do you need the stimulation of others? Does a shared enthusiasm help you to go on? Would the added luxury of saunas, jacuzzis, beauty treatments and refreshments that some gyms provide help you to persevere? Would the advice of a teacher help you, or the discipline of a class make it easier to force yourself to your limits? Again, if training at home, would it help to find a partner (what Americans would call 'a training buddy') to work with you, or are you happy alone? If you decide on training at home, make sure there is room for your apparatus. If you can set aside a room for training, so much the better. If every time you have to get your weights out of the attic or the garage, it only adds to the temptation to put off training on a busy day. If they are there to hand, it is easier to find time and avoid excuses.

Secondly, remember that training should be fun. Serious body builders will need to concentrate on the muscles they are using, and such women are usually dedicated enough to continue without the aid of music or other incentives, but if you are fond of doing things to music there is no reason why some of the rhythmic exercises should not be done in this way. Or if you are using an exercise bike, there is no reason why you should not read a book balanced on your handlebars. Large-print ones are ideal for this purpose.

If figure improvement or body building is your aim, a before and after photograph will encourage you, preferably taken nude. You may need a certain amount of courage to strip for the first one, but when you have the second taken in three months' time, the difference will double your enthusiasm to carry on, and the one you take in a year's time will make it all seem worth while.

The next tip to help you persevere is making a plan. Plan your week, on paper, and set it up before you. People often think they have not got time for things simply because they are disorganised. Write down when you are going to get up, what time breakfast is, when you are going to do the housework, when your other meals and snacks are going to be prepared and eaten, when you are going to bed, and fit into this plan your social activities, your periods of relaxation, and of course your exercise period. If you go out to work, add to this list the times you leave for work and return home. Set up also, in a place that you can see it, your Menu plan for the week, so that you are not constantly having to think about what to get for the next meal. Planning saves time, saves repetitious movements, saves you forgetting anything.

As well as your plan for the week, you will be helped in your training by a progress chart. Set out your weights and measurements as detailed in Chapter 2, with dates and with spaces in your chart to enter improvements month by month. This, like the photo, will encourage you to continue by actually showing you the benefits in black and white. A particularly encouraging chart for slimmers is the graph. Plot weight along the upright of the graph and weeks along the bottom, and as you see the curve of the graph descend you will know that you are on the right path.

If, in spite of these incentives – photos, records, graph – you feel half-hearted, then give yourself rewards. This is how psychologists stimulate animal behaviour. You could even give yourself punishments, as they do to the poor animals, but there is no need to be quite so masochistic. A day out if you keep it up for three months; a new record if you are still doing it next week; a theatre visit if you lose another 4lb. These are tricks, and if husband or boyfriend will help by supplying them, so much the better.

Finally, do not be afraid to talk about your training. Do not bore all your friends, of course, but try to meet people who are also interested, or if any of your particular friends show interest, try to induce them to train too. It will be good for them, and comparing notes will encourage you both. Read all you can about training and about diet. Make your meals as interesting as possible and your training sessions as varied as you can with the apparatus available. All these things help to keep enthusiasm alive.

Finally, have faith in yourself. You will soon be saying: 'I feel good. I can cope with life. I look beautiful.' You will 'walk tall'.

8 Relaxation and Meditation

You may ask what have relaxation and meditation to do with weight training. Weight training is related to total health. If you are healthy and happy, you will more easily achieve your training goals. Relaxation takes away all the physical strains, enabling your body to find true rest, in which its natural tendency to do any repairs and to right itself can function. Meditation is a way of relaxing the mind and spirit.

Stress is one of the ills of modern society and we all suffer from it to a certain extent. It aggravates any tendency to illness; it can make us more accident-prone; it can prevent our giving full attention to weight training because our mind will be on other things. There are many causes of stress. If we live in a city, we have to put up with pollution of the atmosphere, rubbish in the streets, vandalism, noise, bright lights, the bombardment of advertising, high-rise buildings, overcrowding, muggings, burglary, traffic hazards, the speed at which everything goes including life itself, and the loneliness that the lack of a supportive community can bring. If we live in the country, we escape some of the ills of city life, but we can face loneliness and isolation, and may feel deprived of amusements, stylish shops, access to sports, cultural activities and wider job opportunities.

Work is one of the prime causes of stress in life. Some women may feel that they are not given the same opportunities as men, despite legislation, and feel that there is little they can do about it. They may be passed over for promotion; they may have to work under supervisors who are less competent than they are. Some may fear unemployment; they may be very poorly paid, and struggling to make ends meet; they may

have to perform boring and repetitious tasks, and may have no real job satisfaction at all. On the other hand, some women may be given responsibilities greater than their capacity, or they may be called upon to supervise people who let them down.

Housewives face stresses of their own. If they have all the latest labour-saving gadgets, they may be bored with too little to do. If they do not have them, they may envy their friends who do. If they take a job to ease the money situation, they may become over-burdened, particularly if their husband does not take his share of the household tasks to help out.

Mothers at the beck and call of their young children can feel stress too; however rewarding their position, they long for time of their own to develop their own interests — or simply have a moment's peace!

Marriage produces stress, particularly if there is fear or suspicion of unfaithfulness; if the husband is mean over money; if love has flown with the passing years; if there is a divergence of sexual needs. But single women have stresses too.

Relaxation, which really means 'letting go', can help to alleviate stress. Meditation can still the turmoil of thoughts that will not let us rest. Five minutes of each every day will be of great benefit, not only to our general health, but also to our training programme.

To relax physically, find a quiet place, a bedroom, a couch or a shady spot on the lawn. Lie flat on your back. Begin with your toes and gradually work up your legs, relaxing each muscle in turn. Then relax your arms and shoulders, your head and neck, and finally your trunk. Feel as though you are sinking right down through the supporting bed or lawn. Let yourself go, with no tension at all. It helps to achieve this relaxation if you first tense a muscle and then let it relax. Clench your fist tightly. The muscles in your arm bunch up. Now slowly let your hand unfold like a flower, relaxing each finger and each muscle consciously. Flex your biceps and then lower your arm, letting it hang loosely like a rope by your side. Tense your stomach muscles by drawing them in, and then slowly let them relax. In this way, you can work all over your body, recognising the difference between tension and relaxation, until you can fully savour the latter.

Do these exercises in a quiet place, where you will not be distracted; some people find them easier in a subdued light. Be warm enough for comfort but not over-heated. Enjoy a few minutes of physical relaxation whenever you feel the need as well as at a regular time each day.

Relaxation is helped by slow deep breathing. Feel yourself sinking back as you breathe out. Ten deep breaths followed by a return to normal breathing should put you in a suitable physical state to relax. Breathing itself will relax you, without your even lying down, if you have to face a stressful situation. Oxygen calms the nerves. Next time you have to face an important interview or go to the dentist or feel apprehensive about something, take a few deep breaths. You will appreciate their wonderful calming effect.

Meditation is the equivalent of relaxation on a mental or spiritual level. During the 1960's, there was quite a vogue in 'Transcendental Meditation', due in part to the interest shown in it by such groups as The Beatles. Eastern teachers, including the transcendentalists, usually give their students a 'mantra' to chant. The word mantra literally means thought protection. The aim of the mantra is to protect us from our own thoughts. So by concentrating on the repetition of a single, often meaningless, word, all other thoughts are driven from our minds, and we find rest. All the worries, fears, dislikes, anxieties and even hopes that will not leave our minds are driven out. Having

stilled our thoughts in this way, we are led into complete mental relaxation, and it is believed that this will lay us open to the spiritual powers of the Universe.

Of course, it is not necessary to go to an Eastern teacher or chant a mantra. A similar effect can be achieved by turning your thoughts to some happy scene or experience, concentrating on it, and relishing your remembered enjoyment until all else is driven from your consciousness. Then, if you allow it, even that happy memory will fade, leaving you at peace.

This period of meditation should be combined with a period of physical relaxation. The techniques of emptying the mind are necessary, because it is so difficult consciously to will away our worries. Indeed, the effort of trying to do that will in itself make us tense and prevent any true achievement of relaxation.

All teachers recognise, however, that the empty mind has its dangers and can lay us open to evil influences as well as good. That is why some teachers prefer their students only to practise meditation in a group, especially in the beginning. It is perhaps best if we can practise it in the setting of our own religious faith. Mystics of the various religions have practised emptying the mind of all earthly and extraneous thoughts and turning to God, by whatever name they know Him. This lays them open to new understanding, to strength and to peace. The Bible says: 'They that wait on the Lord shall renew their strength'. And again: 'Be still and know that I am God'. If we have any religious faith, we will probably have had some experience of this, however limited, and it is open to all. Meditation is one of the aspects of yoga, but of course you do not have to take up yoga to enjoy its benefits. If you want to look further into the benefits of meditation, you can join a group that will give you help with the practical techniques, and if you do this the supportive friendship of the group will in itself help to alleviate stress. But even if you do not want to go into it this deeply, you can still benefit by trying the simple techniques outlined in this chapter.

Section 2

THE EXERCISES

Important Note: Although all the exercises are grouped in the five chapters of this section, you should on no account try to work through them all. Turn first to Section 3 and select the particular schedule needed for your own individual training purpose.

9 Exercises Without Apparatus

You may ask why exercises without apparatus are included in a book on weight training. The answer is that it is unwise to go straight into any strenuous activity while the body and the muscles are cold, as this can lead to strains. Before starting any exercise programme with weights, therefore, a few exercises without apparatus are done, to warm up. Those given in this chapter will have a limbering-up effect, and will enable you to go into your schedule safely.

As well as warming up before you begin, however, you must think of tapering off at the end. The deep breathing and relaxing exercises (Nos 7 and 8) will enable you to do this. Do exercises 1 to 8 ten times each at the beginning of every training session, and repeat exercises 7 and 8 ten times each at the end.

Exercise 1 Deep Knee Bends

Stand upright with feet normal distance apart, head erect and relaxed, arms hanging at sides. Rise on the toes and do the deep knees bend, at the same time swinging your arms forwards to shoulder level to help you maintain your balance. Go down as far as possible so that you are virtually sitting on your heels, but if you cannot manage this at first, go as far as you can and progress as your limbs become more supple. Breathe in as you go down and out as you come back up. Let your arms drop back to your sides as you come up.

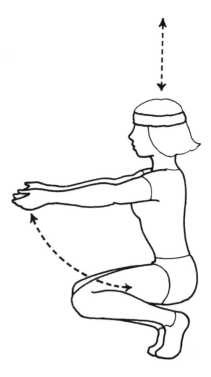

Fig 1

Exercise 2 Touching Floor Between Legs

Stand with feet astride, somewhat wider than normal stance. Take the arms above the head and back. Breathe in deeply. Bend forwards and touch the floor or as far as you can go, between your legs, breathing out as you go down and in as you come back up again. If you cannot touch the floor, you will soon be able to do so with practice.

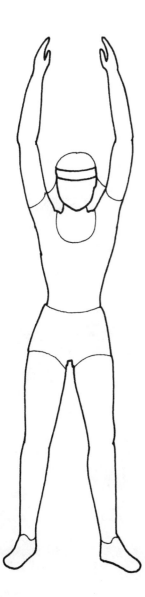

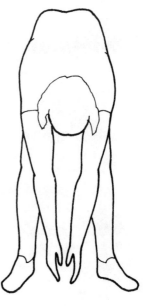

Fig 2

Exercise 3 Trunk Turning

Stand upright, feet a comfortable distance
apart, arms stretched out sideways at
shoulder level as far as possible. Try to keep
your hips still and to turn your trunk as far
to the right as you can. Turn your head and
look to your right rear, and your trunk will
follow. Come back to the front, and im-
mediately turn to the left. Perform the
movement rhythmically from side to side
with a swing.

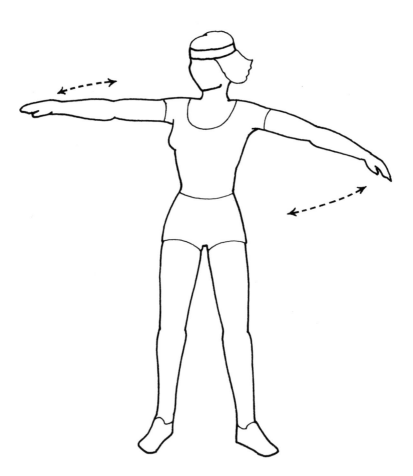

Fig 3

Exercise 4 Side Bends

Stand upright, feet together, hands at sides and palms inwards. With your body facing the front, bend as far over to your right as you can, keeping your knees straight, and letting your palm slide down the side of your right leg. Try to reach as far down as you can with the fingertips. Straighten up and bend over as far as you can to the left in the same way.

Exercise 5 Head Circling

Stand upright, hands at sides, feet together. Bend the head forwards as far as possible, take it to your right shoulder, then up and back, then to your left, forward to your left shoulder, and to the centre again. After 5 circles in this clockwise direction, do 5 in an anti-clockwise direction.

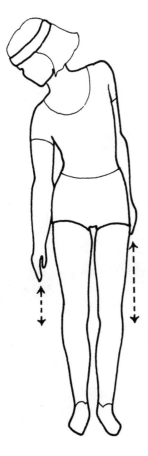

Fig 4

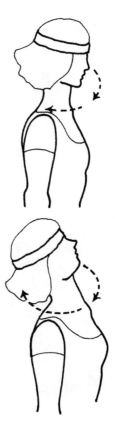

Fig 5

43

Exercise 6 Touching Alternate Toes

Stand with feet wide apart, arms above head. Bend forwards and with the right fingertips touch your left toes. Straighten up, arms above head again, and with the left fingertips touch your right toes. Breathe out as you bend down and in as you straighten up. If you cannot quite make it at first, go down as far as you can, and with increasing suppleness you will soon be able to do the exercise.

Exercise 7 Deep Breathing with Arms and Swinging

Stand upright and relaxed, head up and shoulders back, feet normal distance apart. Cross the arms in front of you. Swing the arms upwards, sideways and backwards, breathing in deeply as you do so. Bring the arms down to the crossed position in front of you, breathing out.

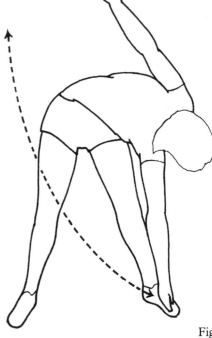

Fig 6

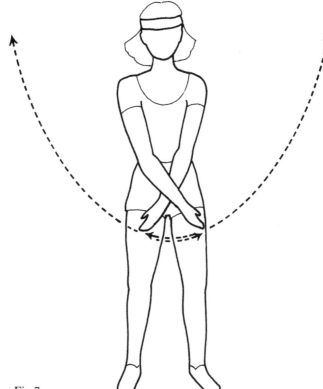

Fig 7

Exercise 8 Relaxing

Stand upright. Let the arms hang loosely at your sides, and shake each in turn, being sure to let the wrist relax and shake that as well. Think of your arm as a rope hanging loosely from your shoulder joint, not stiff at all, and shake it for 10 seconds. Then repeat with the other arm.

Raise one leg off the ground, and letting it hang loosely as you did with the arm, shake that, letting it swing. Repeat with the other leg.

This particular exercise derives from karate practice, and has been found useful in preparing the limbs for the more strenuous training that follows.

Exercise 9 Back Exercises

Kneel on hands and knees as in Figure 9 with the back arched and the head down. Raise the head and lower the back, but do not allow it to become hollow. This particular exercise is a remedial rather than a general one. (See Chapter 20.)

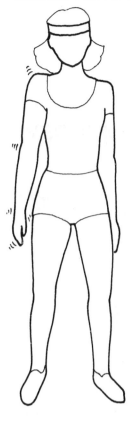

Fig 8

Fig 9

45

10 Exercises with Barbell

In all the exercises in this chapter, refer to Chapter 2 for the weight you should use on the bar.

Exercise 10 Bent Over Rowing

Stand upright, feet normal distance apart. Pick up the bar, hands shoulder-width apart, palms on top of the bar, fingers over, thumbs underneath. Bend forwards until the body is at right angles to the legs and parallel to the ground. Keep the back flat and stay in this forward position with the arms hanging down holding the bar. Now bring the bar up to your chest by bending your elbows, breathing out as you do so. Lower to the hanging position breathing in. Do not put the bar on the ground between repetitions.

This exercise benefits the latissimus dorsi, the trapezius and the triceps, and the deep breathing develops the chest.

Fig 10

Exercise 11 Upright Rowing

Stand upright. Grip the bar with both hands close together near the centre. Make sure that it balances as you lift it. Have your fingers over the bar and thumbs underneath as in Exercise 10. Let the bar hang in front of your thighs. Take a deep breath, and as you breathe out, bring the bar up level with your shoulders, raising the elbows outwards. Try to make the bar touch your chin, and keep it as near the body as possible. Breathe in as you lower to the hanging position. Do not replace the bar on the ground between repetitions.

This exercise is for the deltoids and pectorals.

Exercise 12 Bench Press

Lie on your back on a bench with upper body, shoulders and head firmly supported, and feet on the floor off the end. Take a wide grip on the bar, with fingers over and thumbs under, and the bar resting on your chest, high up, not near your abdomen. With the bar on the chest, take a deep breath, and as you breathe out, push it upwards to arm's length. Breathe in as you lower onto your chest again.

This exercises the whole of the chest area, and is particularly good for the pectorals, triceps and back.

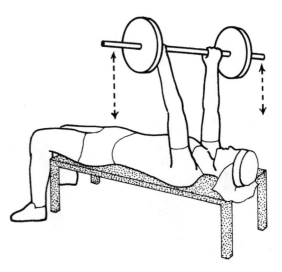

Fig 12

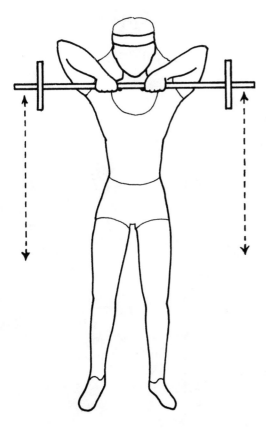

Fig 11

Exercise 13 Clean with Barbell

With the bar on the ground, stand with feet normal distance apart and underneath the bar, toes pointing to the front. Bend your knees and grip the bar with both hands, shoulder-width apart, fingers over and thumbs under the bar. Straighten the knees and lift the bar to a position high across the shoulders in line with the chin. As the bar passes waist level, twist the wrists, so that the weight is mostly on the balls of the thumbs. This movement is done quickly. When the bar is in position across your shoulders, that is called 'the Clean'. Put the bar back on the ground, bending your knees as you do so. Breathe in before you lift, and out as you are lifting.

This exercise is not only for the arms and wrists but also for the leg and back muscles.

Exercise 14 Press with Barbell

From the 'Clean' position described in the last exercise, 'press' the barbell to arm's length above your head. Press slowly and lower slowly to the shoulders again. Breathe out as you press up and in as you lower. Up and down counts as one repetition, and the movement must be done under control.

This exercise is mainly for the biceps and triceps but also helps the back and chest.

Fig 14

Fig 13

Exercise 15 Curls with Barbell

Stand with feet normal distance apart. With hands shoulder-width apart, take the bar in both hands – palms upwards, and let it hang at arm's length down in front of your thighs. From this position, bring the bar up to your chest by bending your arms. Perform the movement slowly, and lower the bar slowly back to the hanging position. Up and down counts as one repetition. Breathe out as you raise the bar, in as you lower.

Exercise 16 Reverse Curls with Barbell

For this exercise you will need a very light weight indeed on the bar. You may even find it sufficient to use the bar alone. Hold the bar behind your body with both hands, palms to the front, so that it rests across your buttocks or the tops of your legs. Keeping the body upright, take the bar back as far as you can. This will only be a few inches, so do not lean forwards to make it more. Having reached that position, turn your wrists back so as to raise the bar away from you. Return to normal with the bar touching your body. Breathe out as you take the bar back, in as you return to normal.

This exercise is for the triceps.

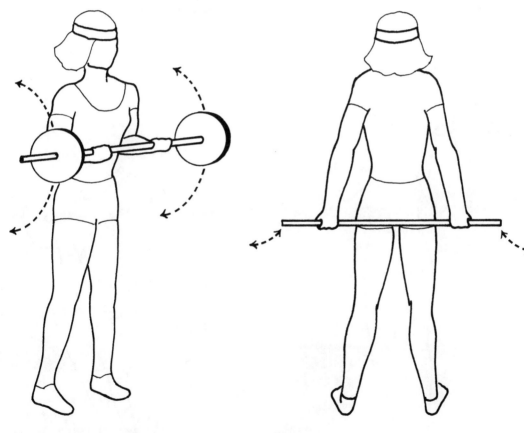

Fig 15   Fig 16

Exercise 17 Press Behind Neck with Barbell

Load the barbell and bring it to the 'Clean' position as in Exercise 13, then take it over the head to rest on the back of the neck. You will need a slightly wider grip with your hands to do this. The palms are to the front, fingers under and curling over the top of the bar. From this position behind the neck, press the bar to arm's length overhead, breathing out as you do so. Lower onto the back of the neck again, breathing in. This counts as one repetition.

The exercise is for the triceps and the erector spinae muscles.

Exercise 18 Squats with Barbell

Take the barbell over your head onto the back of your neck as in the starting position for Exercise 17. From this position, do the deep knees bend, breathing in as you go down and out as you come up. Feet are normal distance apart and heels should remain on the ground.

The exercise is for the legs and the deep breathing involved develops the chest.

Exercise 18(a) Half Squats with Barbell

This is a variation in which you go only half-way down.

Exercise 18(b) Quarter Squats with Barbell

This is a variation going only a little way down.

Fig 17

Fig 18

Exercise 19 Squats with Barbell at Clean

In Exercise 18 the hands were fairly widely spaced because the weight was on the back of the neck. A variation that allows a narrower grip, affecting slightly different muscles, is squatting with the barbell at the 'Clean'. Take the barbell to the 'Clean' as in Exercise 13, and do the deep knees bend from this position. Breathe in as you go down and out as you come up. If you find that the weight tends to unbalance you, put your heels on a low block of wood.

The exercise is for the rectus femoris.

Exercise 20 Heel Raises with Barbell

Take the barbell onto the back of the neck as in Exercise 17. Now, with the barbell in this position, raise the heels, hold the position a few seconds, then lower heels. Breathe out as you raise heels, in as you lower.

Your lower leg muscles benefit.

Fig 19   Fig 20

Exercise 21 Step-up onto Bench with Barbell

Take the barbell on your shoulders as in Exercise 17. Holding it there and in good balance, step up onto a low bench or block of wood, then down again. Breathe out as you step up, in as you step down.

All the leg muscles and the knee joint benefit.

Exercise 22 Good Morning Exercise with Barbell

Take the barbell on the shoulders as in Exercise 17, with feet fairly wide apart. From this position, bend forwards from the waist as far as you can without losing balance, trying to bring the chest at right angles to the legs. Keep the head up. Breathe out as you go down, in as you return to upright.

This exercise is for the trunk and lower back.

Fig 22

Fig 21

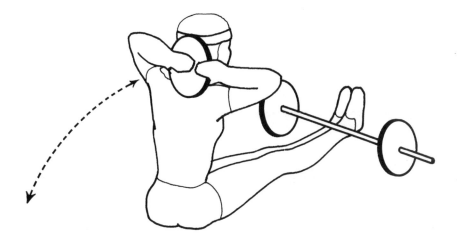

Fig 23

Exercise 23 Sit-ups with Weight

Lie flat on your back on the floor. Tuck your feet under a barbell to stop them coming up. Take one of the disc weights and hold it behind your head with both hands. Now sit up, keeping your legs straight and pulling on the weight at the back of your head to keep it in contact with your head. The exercise is really the simple sit-up, made harder by the extra weight you are bringing up. Breathe out as you sit up, in as you go back down. Control the movement and do not simply flop back.

The upper abdominals benefit most.

Exercise 24 Trunk Turning with Bar on Shoulders

Take the bar on the shoulders as in Exercise 17. Feet are a comfortable distance apart. Try to keep the hips steady and turn from the waist as far to the right as possible, letting the head turn and the bar follow in line with the shoulders. Return to face front, and then turn to your left as far as possible. The bar keeps shoulders and arms in line.

This exercise uses all the muscles around the hips and down the sides of the body.

Fig 24

11 Exercises with Dumb-bells

Refer to Chapter 2 for the weight to use.

Exercise 25 Crucifix with Dumb-bells

Lie on your back on a bench as in Exercise 12, feet firmly on the floor. Take a dumb-bell in each hand, and hold the arms out sideways at shoulder level. Take a deep breath, and as you breathe out, raise the dumb-bells at arm's length in front of the chest. Keep your arms straight. Breathe in as you lower to your sides again. Do not let the weight drop back behind the shoulders.

This exercise is for the pectorals.

Exercise 26 Straight Arm Pull-overs

Load the weight onto the centre of the dumb-bell rod, securing with a collar either side. Lie on the bench as for Exercise 25, with head near the end. Grip the dumb-bell rod at each end and hold it as far down your body as you can with palms facing your feet, so that the fingers curl over the top. Keeping arms straight, take the dumb-bell over your head and behind your body as far as you can, breathing in as you do so. Then bring it forwards again with arms straight, right down your body to your thighs, breathing out. Make sure your hips do not leave the bench, and do not sit up.

This is for the pectorals, the shoulder muscles and the rib cage.

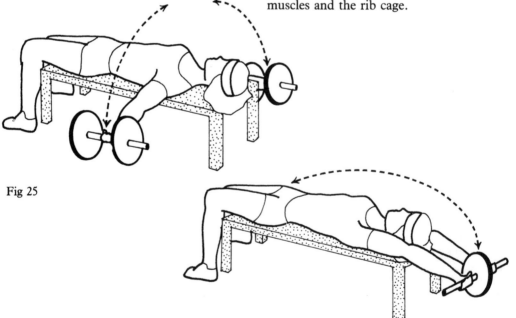

Fig 25

Fig 26

Exercise 27 Bent Arm Pull-overs

Load the dumb-bell centrally, securing with a collar each side. Lie on the bench as for Exercise 26. Grip the dumb-bell with as narrow a grip as possible, and hold it above your chest with elbows bent, upper arms vertical, forearms at right angles and palms facing your head. Lower the dumb-bell over your head by bending your elbows. Breathe in as you do so. Then bring the weight back to the starting position over your chest, breathing out as you do so. Keep the arms bent at the elbows throughout. This is what is called a 'short range movement' unlike Exercise 26 which is 'full range'.

It benefits the triceps and the chest.

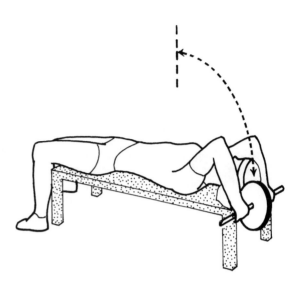

Fig 27

Exercise 28 Alternate Dumb-bell Presses

Stand with feet spaced normally apart. Take a dumb-bell in each hand and bring them up to rest on your shoulders. Press the right hand as high above your head as you can, and as you bring it down to the shoulder again, press the left hand above the head. Breathe freely as you are doing this exercise. Keep the body upright, and to maintain good balance keep the dumb-bells as near the head as you can.

This is for the upper back muscles, the deltoids and the chest.

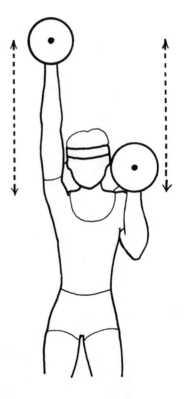

Fig 28

55

Exercise 29 Lateral Raises

Stand with feet astride. Take a dumb-bell in each hand and let them hang down at the sides, palms in towards the body. Raise your arms out to your sides until they are level with your waist, and at this point turn your wrists so that your palms are upwards, and carry on the movement, raising the dumb-bells above the head, when the palms will be facing inwards towards each other. Breathe out as you raise, in as you lower again. Make the turn of the wrists at waist level in raising and in lowering.

This is a full-range movement for the deltoids and latissimus dorsi.

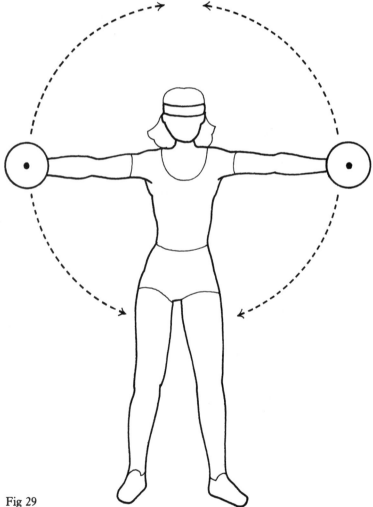

Fig 29

Exercise 30 Forwards and Upwards Swing with Dumb-bells

Stand upright, feet normal distance apart. Take a dumb-bell in each hand letting them hang in front touching the thighs, palms facing the body, knuckles away from you. Raise each dumb-bell alternately, forwards and upwards to shoulder level and then on to above your head, in one continuous movement. As you lower one hand, raise the other. Breathe freely.

This is for the pectorals and all the shoulder muscles.

Exercise 31 Single Hand Rowing with Dumb-bell

Lean forwards from the waist and rest one hand on a bench, table or the back of a chair. Take a dumb-bell in the other hand, palm towards your body, and let it hang down at arm's length. Bring it up to the shoulder level by bending your arm, breathing out as you pull it up and in as you lower it again. Stay in the bent-over position, and after doing a set with one hand, change hands and do a set with the other.

This exercise is for the latissimus dorsi.

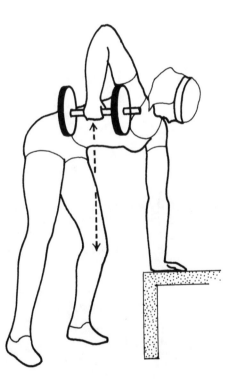

Fig 31

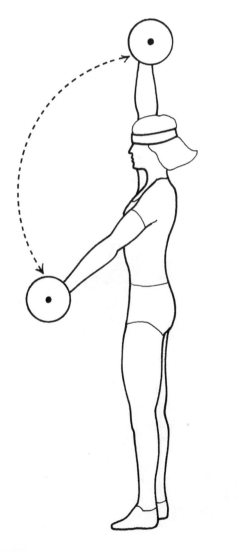

Fig 30

Exercise 32 Triceps Stretch Standing

Load the dumb-bell centrally, with a collar each side to hold the weight in place. Hold in both hands above the head with knuckles to the front, palms to the rear. By bending the elbows, lower the dumb-bell behind the head, and then bring it back to the overhead position again. The upper arms remain straight and upright; it is only the elbows that bend. Breathe in as you lower, out as you raise.

This exercise is for the triceps.

Exercise 33 Triceps Stretch Seated

Load the dumb-bell normally, not centrally, so that you can grip it in the centre. Take it in your right hand. Sit on a bench. Raise the dumb-bell to arm's length overhead, knuckles to the front, palm to the rear. Support your upper arm with your left hand. Lower the dumb-bell behind you by bending your right elbow, maintaining the upper arm vertical. Raise the dumb-bell to arm's length again. Breathe in as you lower it and out as you raise it. Having done the exercise with the right hand, change hands and repeat with the left.

This is for the triceps.

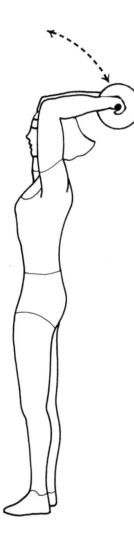

Fig 32

Fig 33

Exercise 34 Single Arm Dumb-bell Curls

Take a loaded dumb-bell in the left hand, palm upwards. Let it hang down at arm's length in front of you, as you stand with feet normal distance apart. Bring it to your shoulder, by bending your left elbow. Breathe out as you bring it up, in as you lower to arm's length again. It helps either to keep the right hand at the side, or to take it behind you. When you have done a set with your left hand, change hands and do a set with your right.

The exercise is for both biceps and triceps.

Exercise 35 Dumb-bell Raises

Stand with feet a comfortable distance apart. Take a dumb-bell in the right hand, knuckles uppermost. Let it hang down at arm's length in front of you. Keep the other hand by your side. Slowly raise the dumb-bell forwards and upwards, keeping your arm straight, until it is at shoulder level and out at arm's length in front of you. Breathe out as you raise. Lower slowly, breathing in. Do a set with the right hand, then change hands and do a set with the left.

All the arm muscles and the deltoids benefit.

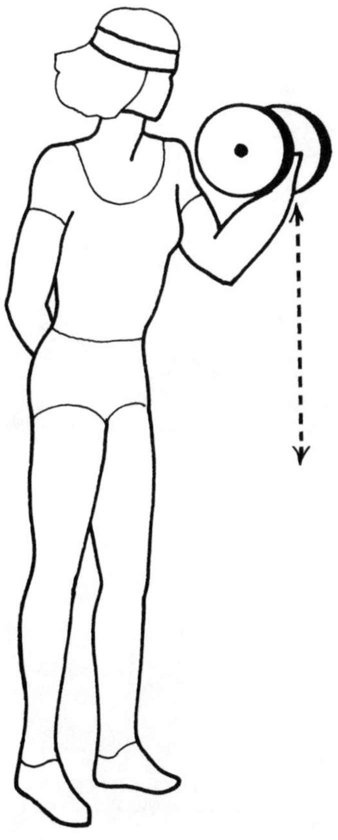

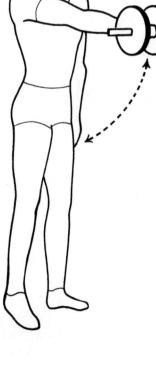

Fig 34

Fig 35

Exercise 36 Side Bends with Dumb-bells

Take a loaded dumb-bell in each hand and stand with feet normal distance apart. Bend as far sideways as you can to your left, letting the dumb-bell slide down the side of your left leg, and curling the one in your right hand up under your armpit. Then bend as far as you can to your right, letting the right hand slide down your right leg and the left curl up under your armpit. Continue bending from side to side and breathing freely.

This exercise is for the external oblique abdominals and for the tensors.

Exercise 37 Trunk Turning with Dumb-bells

Stand feet astride. Take a loaded dumb-bell in each hand and hold arms out to the side in line with the shoulders. Try to keep the hips steady and to turn from the waist as far to your right as possible, turning your head and taking your right arm back and your left one forwards so that your arms holding the dumb-bells form a straight line with your shoulders. Turn to face the front again, and continue turning straight round to your left as far as you can go. Keep turning from side to side and breathing freely.

This is for the trunk muscles.

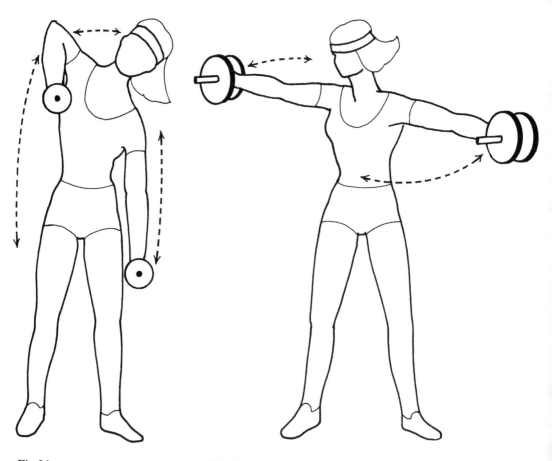

Fig 36   Fig 37

Exercise 38 Squats with Dumb-bells at Shoulders

Stand with feet a comfortable distance apart. Take a loaded dumb-bell in each hand, and bring them to your shoulders. With the dumb-bells held in this position, do the deep knees bend, breathing in. Come up again, breathing out. Keep the dumb-bells in the same position throughout the exercise.

Legs, arms and chest all benefit.

Exercise 39 Side Bends with Dumb-bell Overhead

Load the dumb-bell centrally, securing with a collar each side. Grasp it on either side, with hands straight up above your head, fingers curled over the top of the rod, palms to the front. Stand with feet normal distance apart. Bend as far as you can to your right, keeping your knees straight, and then straighten up and bend as far as you can to your left. Breathe freely.

This is one of the strongest exercises for the muscles of the trunk.

Fig 38

Fig 39

12 Exercises With Other Apparatus

Again, if weights are involved, refer to Chapter 2.

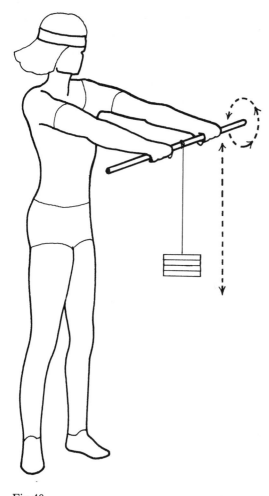

Fig 40

62

Exercise 40 Wrist Roller Exercise

Take the rod with a weight attached to the string in both hands, palms downwards, and hold it out in front of you at shoulder level or just below. Then raise the weight by turning the rod towards you and so winding up the string around it.

It benefits not only the wrists but the whole of the forearms.

Exercise 41 Iron Boots Leg Raise Sideways

For this you need iron boots on your feet. If you have not got any, use heavy shoes, or attach sandbags to your shoes to add extra weight. Stand by a wall, resting your right hand against it. Put your left hand on your left hip. Raise your left leg sideways as far as you can, breathing out as you raise. Lower again, breathing in. Complete a set with the left leg, before turning round to put the other hand against the wall and repeating with the other leg.

This benefits the tensor muscles, the vastus externus and all the hip and leg muscles.

Exercise 42 Iron Boots Leg Raise Backwards

Stand facing a wall. Place both hands against it, body upright. Raise your left leg backwards, by bending the knee, with the iron boot on. Breathe out as you raise and in as you lower again. Do a set of repetitions with your left leg, then repeat with the right.

The biceps of the leg benefit.

Fig 41

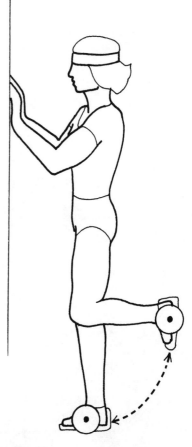

Fig 42

Exercise 43 Iron Boots Leg Swing

Stand sideways to a wall as in Exercise 41. Rest your left hand on the wall and your right on your hip. Swing your right leg backwards and forwards, with the iron boot on, breathing freely. Change to right hand on wall, left on hip, and swing the left leg backwards and forwards. Keep the leg straight in each case, and swing loosely from the hip.

This exercises the hips and buttocks.

Exercise 44 Iron Boots Knee Raises

Stand with your back to a wall, hands on hips. With iron boots on, raise alternate knees as high in front of you as you can, and lower slowly. Breathe out as you raise and in as you lower.

This is excellent for upper leg and abdominal muscles.

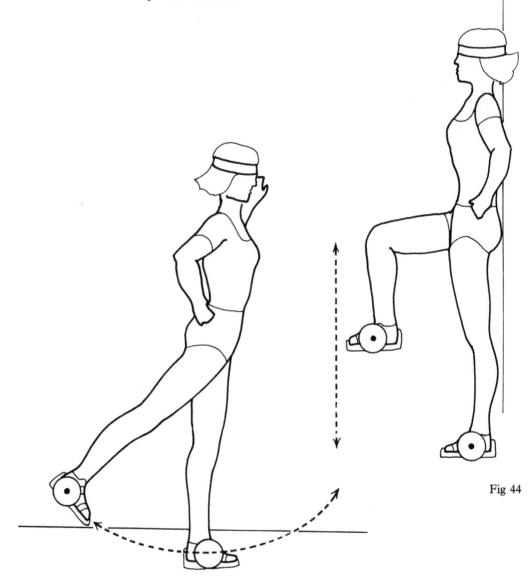

Fig 44

Fig 43

Exercise 45 Iron Boots Thigh Extension

Sit on a bench or table high enough for both legs to hang without touching the ground. Wearing iron boots, raise each leg alternately straight out in front of you, and lower to the hanging position again.

This benefits the leg muscles and the knee joint.

Exercise 46 Knee Raises with Iron Boots from Prone Position

Lie on your back, wearing iron boots. Your hands, palms down, on the floor at your sides give you some support. Raise both knees together as high as you can towards your chest. Breathe out as you raise them, and in as you take your legs back to the ground.

This benefits the leg muscles and the abdominals.

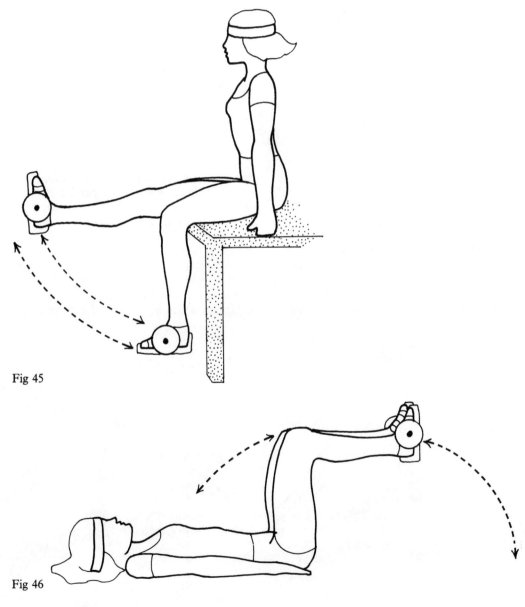

Fig 45

Fig 46

Exercise 47 Leg Raises with Iron Boots from Prone Position

Lie on your back, wearing iron boots, hands clenched behind your head touching the floor. Raise each leg in turn, keeping it straight. Breathe out as you raise and in as you lower. You can vary the exercise by raising both legs together, and you will find that this is slightly easier.

Leg and abdominal muscles benefit.

Fig 47

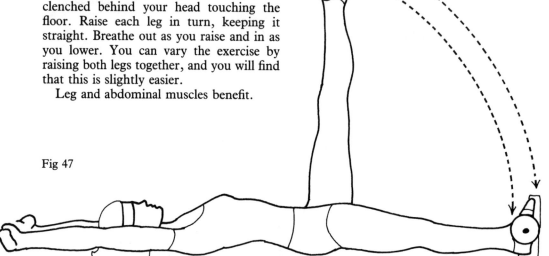

Exercise 48 Sit-ups with Weight on Incline Bench

This is only possible if you have one of the benches that can be set at varying angles. Do not worry if you do not have this apparatus. Substitute Exercise 23 from Chapter 10 instead.

At the top of the incline bench is a strap. Tuck your feet in this to hold them securely. Lie head downwards. Hold a round disc weight to the back of your head with both hands. Now sit up and try to touch your knees with your nose, breathing out as you sit up, and in as you lower yourself back down. The angle of the bench will determine how hard it is, and to exercise harder as you progress, you can either alter the angle or increase the weight, or both.

This is a strong abdominal exercise.

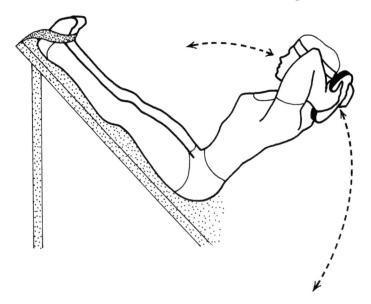

Fig 48

Fig 49

Exercise 49 Rowing Machine

This is for those who have the apparatus. Sit on the seat, press your feet against the foot supports, take the handles in your hands, and row. The seat slides back and forth as you do so. Breathe in as you go back, and out as you come forwards.

The leg, arm, stomach and back muscles all benefit.

Exercise 50 Exercise Bike

This is for those who have the apparatus. Set the resistance to what you want. Sit in the saddle, grasp the handlebars, and cycle, breathing freely.

The legs and abdominal muscles benefit.

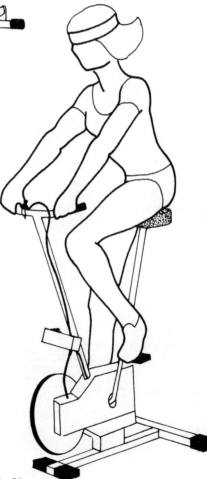

Fig 50

13 Exercises with Machines

The exercises in this chapter are those you can do with the machines in a leisure centre. Do not attempt to do them all at once, but refer to Section 3 and select the schedule needed for your particular purpose.

Exercise 51 Leg Press

Sit with your back firmly against the seat, hands holding the seat rail. Breathe in. Press feet firmly against the pedals, and extend the legs as far as possible, breathing out as you do so. Return to the starting position, keeping the tension on the weights.

This benefits the thigh and hip muscles.

Exercise 52 Hip Flexor

Rest the arms on the forearm supports, and grasp the hand grips. Breathe in, and pull the knees to the chest as you are breathing out. Roll your hips forwards to bring your knees as high as possible. Control the action all the way up and down, flexing the abdominals as much as possible. Breathe in as you lower the legs to the starting position.

This is for the abdominal and hip flexor muscles.

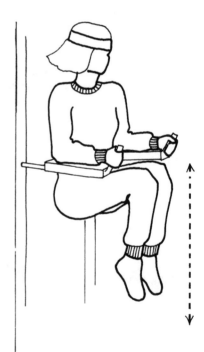

Fig 52

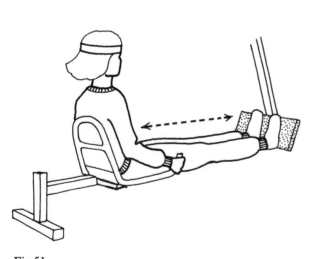

Fig 51

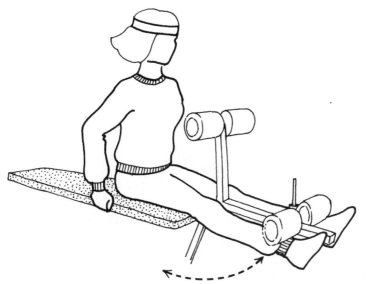

Fig 53

Exercise 53 Thigh and Knee Leg Extension

Sit on the machine and grasp sides of seat or the handrails. Lock the ankles under the rollers; do not point the toes. Breathe in at the start, and while you lift the legs upwards to the full extension, breathe out. Flex the thighs and hold the extension for 1 second. Breathe in as you lower the weights to the starting position.

This is for the knee joint and leg muscles.

Exercise 54 High Pulley

Grasp the bar with a wide grip. Kneel on floor or sit on a low stool, directly under the pulley. Keep the back straight. Breathe out as you pull the bar to either your chest or the back of the head. Breathe in as you let the bar and the weights go back. Let the arms stretch to their complete extension. Do the pulls alternately to the chest and then to behind the head.

This exercises the pectorals, the latissimus dorsi and the arm muscles.

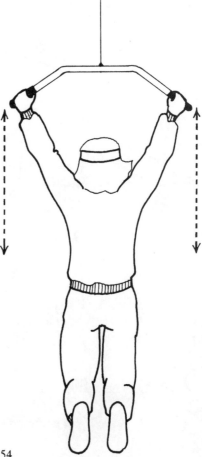

Fig 54

Exercise 55 Rowing

Sit upright, with soles of feet against the machine bar. Grip the handles, and pull elbows to shoulder level as you breathe out. Slowly release the tension as you breathe in, leaning forwards as the hands go back.

This benefits the deltoids, pectorals, trapezius, latissimus dorsi and abdominals.

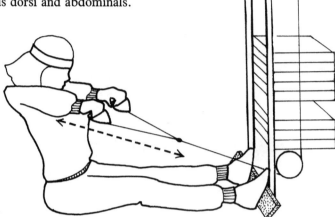

Fig 55

Exercise 56 Low Pulley Thigh Pulls

Stand with your right side to the machine, your left foot in the strap. Raise the left leg sideways as far as you can, breathing out, and breathe in as you return the leg to normal. Now face the opposite way, and still with the strap on your left leg cross your left leg over your right, breathing out as you are crossing your leg, and in as you are lowering. Repeat the whole exercise with the strap on the other ankle.

The first movement exercises the muscles on the outside of the leg; the second the muscles on the inside.

Fig 56

Exercise 57 Dead Lift

Stand upright facing the machine. Grasp the handles. Start pulling upwards with elbows high, taking them towards the ceiling. Breathe out as you raise the hands to your chin. Lower slowly, breathing in.

This strengthens the trapezius, the deltoids, the rhomboids and all the muscles of the chest area.

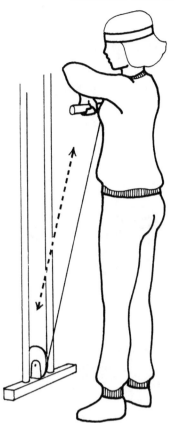

Exercise 58 Abdominal Conditioner Sit-ups

Lie on the board with your insteps under the rollers, knees bent. Clasp hands behind head. Sit up and bring first your right elbow to your left knee, and then your left elbow to your right knee. Breathe in as you lower yourself back to the starting position each time, and out as you come up to touch knees in turn.

This is for the abdominal and hip flexor muscles.

Fig 57

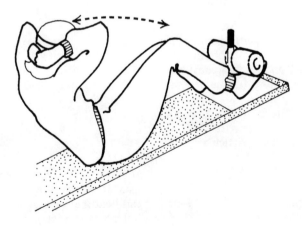

Fig 58

Exercise 59 Chest Press

Fig 59

Lie flat on the bench with feet on the floor. Grasp the handles, keeping elbows in close to the body, and push handles upwards. Breathe out as you push up, in as you lower again.

The exercise is for the pectorals, deltoids and triceps.

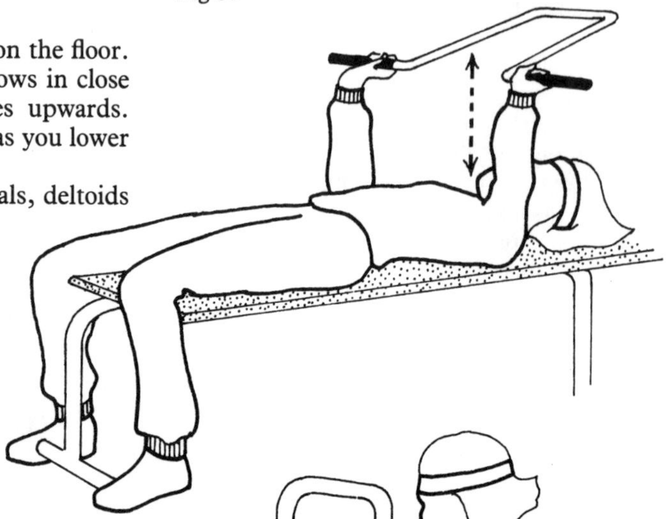

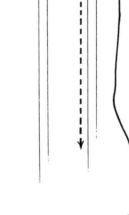

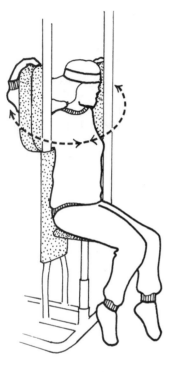

Fig 60

Exercise 60 Chest Bench

Lift the arms and put them around the blocks to grip them in the most comfortable position. Keep head and back against the pads. Breathe in, and as you breathe out, concentrate on forcing the elbows together. Breathe in as you return to the starting position.

This is for the chest and particularly the pectorals.

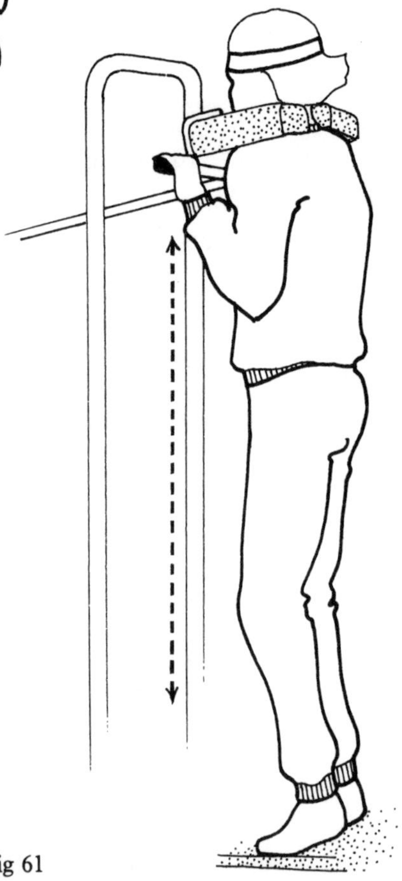

Fig 61

Exercise 61 Leg Squat

Position yourself under the pads with knees bent. Grasp the handles. The action consists in straightening your knees against the resistance of the weights as you breathe out, and bending them again as you breathe in.

This is for the gluteus maximus, the gluteus medius, the erector spinae and the rectus abdominus muscles.

Exercise 62 Dipping

Place hands on the hand grips. Breathe in, and as you breathe out lift the body clear of the ground until the arms are supporting you with elbows straight, then bend the knees at right angles. Breathe in as you lower your body and feet to the ground again.

This is for the deltoids, pectorals and trapezius.

Exercise 63 Chinning

Place hands on the hand grips. Breathe in, and as you breathe out, raise your body to bring your head above the bar, bending your elbows to do so. Hold position a second, and breathe in as you lower yourself back to the floor.

This is for the deltoids, biceps, triceps, pectorals and trapezius.

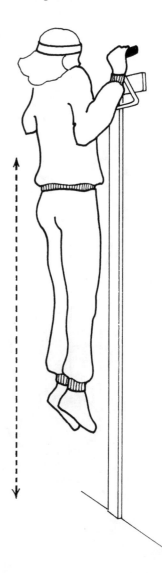

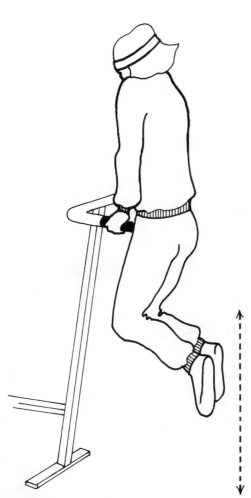

Fig 62

Fig 63

Exercise 64 Standing Twister

Stand on the turntable, hold the rail with both hands, and twist the lower body first to one side and then to the other, keeping the upper body in line with the shoulders and hands. Breathe freely.

This firms and shapes the waist and upper torso, and conditions the back muscles.

Exercise 65 Seated Twister

Sit on the revolving stool and hold the rail with both hands. Twist the lower body first to one side and then to the other, keeping the upper body and shoulders facing the rail in line with the hands. Breathe freely.

This firms and shapes the waist and upper torso, and conditions the back muscles, and is a variation of Exercise 64.

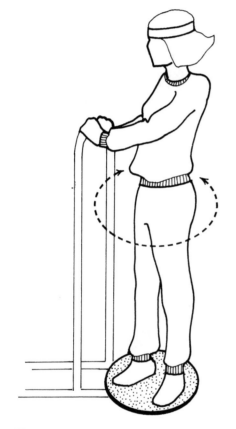

Fig 64

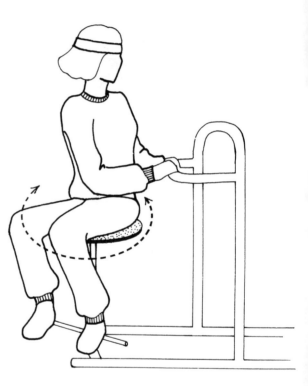

Fig 65

THE TRAINING SCHEDULES

Warning: Do not attempt to do all these exercises. Choose the section appropriate to your particular purpose and study the information on how and when to train given in Chapter 2.

To get the maximum from your training you should study the whole of Section 1 first, and make sure you are combining your training with the correct diet.

If you suffer from any medical condition consult your doctor before starting any training, as in some cases even such simple exercises as deep breathing can be harmful.

14 For General Fitness

General fitness or keeping fit is probably the most common reason for taking up any exercise. Not everyone wants to develop their physique or to train for a sport, but everyone wants ordinary good health, and exercise can contribute so much to this end. You may take up some sport, or go in for jogging or cycling, but the drawback to these methods is that you exercise one group of muscles more than another. For fitness, you need all-round exercise that uses every muscle group in turn, and this is where a planned weight-training schedule has the advantage.

If your aim is the development of your physique, building any under-developed muscles, figure trimming or slimming, go on to the chapters that deal with these matters. The schedules here are not designed for any of those purposes; the course in this chapter has the one simple aim: ordinary fitness for the ordinary woman.

It will only be necessary to do one set of each of the exercises, not two or three sets as required for development. The scheme can be followed every day since it is not over-exhausting, though you may feel stiff after the first time or two. Do not worry about that; the stiffness will go in a week or so. The routine will not take you more than half an hour.

In order to keep up your enthusiasm it is best not to overload yourself with work, so apart from warming up, only eight exercises have been chosen. Although it is clearly best to work at home with barbell and dumb-bells, substituting when you have only dumb-bells as indicated, a parallel course that could be followed at a leisure centre with the apparatus there is also given. If you do decide to go to a leisure centre for this simple keep-fit work-out, you may not want to go every night, even if you could book the centre that often, but every other night would make sure that you were getting your exercise in regular doses.

As mentioned in Chapter 9, you must always warm up first, and relax at the end.

Your Training Schedule at Home
Exercises 1 to 8 without apparatus. 10 repetitions each.
Exercise 18 Squats with Barbell. 10 repetitions.
Exercise 15 Curls with Barbell. 10 repetitions.
Exercise 16 Reverse Curls with Barbell. 10 repetitions.
Exercise 14 Press with Barbell. 10 repetitions.
Exercise 10 Bent Over Rowing with Barbell. 10 repetitions.
Exercise 23 Sit-ups with Weight. 10 repetitions.
Exercise 47 Leg Raises. 10 repetitions. (Heavy shoes will suffice instead of iron boots.)
Exercise 12 Bench Press. 10 repetitions.
Exercises 7 and 8 to cool down. 10 repetitions of each.
For this routine, use a light poundage, so that you are not straining, even on the last repetition. If, after a few months, it becomes too easy, add slightly to your poundage, rather than increase the number of repetitions, since doing that would mean that your routine would take too long to get through. You can spare half an hour a day for fitness; you are unlikely to spend an hour and a half for more than a very limited period.

If you do not have a barbell, only dumb-

bells, make the following substitutions:
For **Exercise 18** do **Exercise 38**
For **Exercise 15** do **Exercise 34**
For **Exercise 16** do **Exercise 32**
For **Exercise 14** do **Exercise 28**
For **Exercise 10** do **Exercise 31**
For **Exercise 12** do **Exercise 25**
Exercises 23 and 47 would be the same.

If you have both barbell and dumb-bells you can vary your routine by substituting exercises as above at will, and this is a valuable trick to avoid staleness and boredom creeping in.

Your Training Schedule at a Leisure Centre
Exercises 1 to 8 without apparatus. 10 repetitions each.
Exercise 61 Leg Squat. 10 repetitions.
Exercise 54 High Pulley. 10 repetitions.
Exercise 63 Chinning. 10 repetitions.
Exercise 58 Sit-ups. 10 repetitions.
Exercise 62 Dipping. 10 repetitions.

Exercise 56 Low Pulley Thigh Pulls. 10 repetitions.
Exercise 55 Rowing. 10 repetitions.
Exercise 59 Chest Press. 10 repetitions.
Exercises 7 and 8 to cool down. 10 repetitions of each.

No one would pretend that such a simple routine will develop muscle. Its purpose is simply to make sure you regularly use the muscles you have got, since muscles not used tend to atrophy. This course will keep you fit; it will overcome tired feelings; and it will put you on top of the world.

Many women who are already overburdened with work find it hard to believe that further work in the form of exercise will do them any good. They would protest that they are already doing enough. But what they do probably only uses the same few muscles in their body; it becomes dreary because they have to do it; and they are without the incentive that a programme designed for total health would give them.

15 For Slimming

It is useless to rely on exercise alone if you wish to slim. It is equally unprofitable to rely on diet alone, since your metabolic rate (the rate at which you use up your food intake) will slow down with your reduced diet, and you will soon be back where you started. To slim successfully, you need both exercise and diet.

Consult Chapter 5 for a suitable diet; follow one of the schedules in this chapter for your exercises.

There are three points to be considered if you are training for this specific purpose:

1 You must use low weights and high repetitions, avoiding at all costs going on to the 'point of resistance', since this would build you up, not reduce you.

2 Your routine must cover all your muscle groups. You may think that if you have a roll of fat around your middle that you can get rid of it with plenty of hip and abdominal exercises. This is a fallacy. It is true that you could firm up your muscles and your fat would sag less so you might look a bit better, but the fat which exercise burns off comes from all over your body, and not just the specific parts used in the exercise.

3 Non-static exercises are better for slimmers than static ones, hence jogging or cycling or a sport like squash would help more than a routine in a gym. So although we give a weight-training schedule to be followed on alternate nights, if you can go out jogging or play some energetic game on the nights in between, you will accelerate your progress.

Your Schedule at Home
Exercises 1 to 8 10 repetitions each.
Exercise 18 Squats with Barbell. 10 increasing to 20.

Exercise 28 Alternate Dumb-bell Presses. 10 each hand increasing to 20 each hand.
Exercise 26 Straight Arm Pull-overs. 10 increasing to 20.
Exercise 11 Upright Rowing. 10 increasing to 20.
Exercise 25 Crucifix with Dumb-bells. 10 increasing to 15.
Exercise 37 Trunk Turning with Dumb-bells. Use 5lb dumb-bells. 20 each way increasing to 50 each way.
Exercise 36 Side Bends with Dumb-bells. Use 5lb dumb-bells. 20 each side working up to 50 each side.
Exercise 23 Sit-ups. Do without weight. 15 increasing to 50, split into more than 1 set, if you like.
Exercise 47 Leg Raises from Prone Position. Do without iron boots. 15 increasing to 30.
Exercise 22 Good Morning Exercise with Barbell. Use very light weight, perhaps bar only to begin with. 10 increasing to 20.
Exercises 7 and 8 to cool down. 10 repetitions each.

If you are without a barbell, substitute dumb-bell exercises instead. Rest a minute between each exercise.

When you have been training for six weeks, make two intervals in the above schedule, one after **Exercise 25**, the other after **Exercise 23**. In these intervals, either use the Exercise Bike (**Exercise 50**) or the Rowing Machine (**Exercise 49**), or if you have not got either, run on the spot or skip for 3 minutes before returning to your schedule.

Your Schedule at a Leisure Centre
Exercise 1 to 8 to warm up. 10 repetitions each.

Exercise 61 Leg Squats. 10 increasing to 20.

Exercise 53 Thigh and Knee Leg Extension. 20 increasing to 40.

Exercise 63 Chinning. 10 increasing to 30.

Exercise 60 Chest Bench. 10 increasing to 25.

Exercise 59 Chest Press. 10 increasing to 25.

Exercise 64 Standing Twister. 15 increasing to 30.

Exercise 65 Seated Twister. 15 increasing to 30.

Exercise 58 Abdominal Conditioner Sit-ups. 30 increasing to 50.

Exercise 56 Low Pulley Thigh Pulls. 20 increasing to 30.

Exercise 52 Hip Flexor. 20 increasing to 25.

Exercises 7 and 8 to cool down. 10 repetitions each.

Increase the number of repetitions gradually to suit yourself, and at no time work to the point of exhaustion. Use very light poundages on the machines.

After six weeks, make two intervals, one after **Exercise 63** and the other after **Exercise 64**, and in these intervals do 3 minutes on the Exercise Bike (**Exercise 50**) or the Rowing Machine (**Exercise 49**).

No doubt, if you are a keen slimmer, you will be keeping records of progress. There is one fact to bear in mind. Exercise builds muscle, and muscle is heavier than fat, so you must not rely on the scales alone to assess results; you must rely on your tape measure. In slimming clinics, fat is measured by taking loose flesh between callipers. Gather up a roll of flesh around your middle between your thumb and fingers. If you can pick up more than an inch, you are too fat, regardless of your weight.

Of course, weight reduction is important, but do not be surprised to see a slight increase in the beginning as fat is replaced by muscle. In spite of this, you will begin to look slimmer, and as your diet takes effect your desired weight loss will come about.

16 For Figure Trimming

Are you dissatisfied with your figure, either because it has failed to develop proportionately or because it has gone to seed? Perhaps you have thin arms and fat legs; perhaps your stomach sags forward, or your bust is nearly non-existent. Weight training cannot work miracles. Once you have passed the age of twenty-six your bones have reached their full development, and then you can only build on the skeletal structure you already have, but none the less you can make some improvement which, with attention to posture, will transform your appearance.

First, you must understand that it is unwise to plunge into exercising one group of muscles only, the ones that you feel need developing. Any specialisation should form part of an all-round course. Follow, therefore, the short all-round course below, and add the extra exercises for the particular development you are seeking. Do the routine every other night.

Your Schedule at Home
Basic all-round routine
Exercises 1 to 8 to warm up. 10 repetitions each.
Exercise 35 Dumb-bell Raises. 2 × 10. (For an explanation of 2 × 10 refer back to page 16.)
Exercise 18 Squats with Barbell. 2 × 10.
Exercise 26 Straight Arm Pull-overs. 2 × 10.
Exercise 22 Good Morning Exercise with Barbell. 2 × 10.
(This will strengthen your back muscles before you start overhead lifts.)
Exercise 36 Side Bends with Dumb-bells. 2 × 10 each side.
Exercise 47 Leg Raises from Prone Position, but without iron boots. 2 × 15.
Exercise 23 Sit-ups with Weight. 2 × 15.
Exercise 20 Heel Raises with Barbell. 2 × 10.

After 6 weeks, when the back is stronger, add:
Exercise 14 Press with Barbell. 2 × 10.
To the above general schedule add those of the following exercises that you specifically need.

For Abdominals (slack stomach muscles)
Exercise 37 Trunk Turning with Dumb-bells. 2 × 10 increasing to 3 × 15, each side.
Exercise 44 Iron Boots Knee Raises. 2 × 10 increasing to 3 × 15.
Exercise 47 Leg Raises with Iron Boots from Prone Position. 2 × 10 increasing to 3 × 15.
Exercise 48 Sit-ups with Weight on Incline Bench. 2 × 10 increasing to 3 × 15.
In the above, if you do not have iron boots, use heavy shoes; if you do not have an incline bench, substitute **Exercise 23**.
Exercise 39 Side Bends with Dumb-bell Overhead. 2 × 10 increasing to 3 × 15.

For Leg Development
Exercise 19 Squats with Barbell at Clean. 2 × 10 increasing to 3 × 15.
Exercise 21 Step-up onto Bench with Barbell. 2 × 10 increasing to 3 × 15.
Exercise 38 Squats with Dumb-bells at Shoulder. 2 × 10 increasing to 3 × 15.
Exercise 41 Iron Boots Leg Raise Sideways. 2 × 10 increasing to 3 × 15.
Exercise 42 Iron Boots Leg Raise Backwards. 2 × 10 increasing to 3 × 15.
Exercise 43 Iron Boots Leg Swing. 2 × 10 increasing to 3 × 15.

Exercise 45 Iron Boots Thigh Extension. 2 × 10 increasing to 3 × 15.
(If you do not have iron boots, use heavy shoes.)

For Arm Development
Exercise 10 Bent Over Rowing. 2 × 10 increasing to 3 × 15.
Exercise 11 Upright Rowing. 2 × 10 increasing to 3 × 15.
Exercise 15 Curls with Barbell. 2 × 10 increasing to 3 × 15.
Exercise 16 Reverse Curls with Barbell. 2 × 10 increasing to 3 × 15.
Exercise 26 Straight Arm Pull-overs. 2 × 10 increasing to 3 × 15.
Exercise 32 Triceps Stretch Standing. 2 × 10 increasing to 3 × 15.
(On alternate weeks, do **Exercise 33** Triceps Stretch Seated, instead.)
Exercise 40 Wrist Roller Exercise. Wind up 3 times.

For the Chest
Exercise 12 Bench Press. 2 × 10 increasing to 3 × 15.
Exercise 13 Clean with Barbell. 2 × 10 increasing to 3 × 15.
Exercise 29 Lateral Raises. 2 × 10 increasing to 3 × 15
Exercise 30 Forwards and Upwards Swing with Dumb-bells. 2 × 10 increasing to 3 × 15.
Exercise 26 Straight Arm Pull-overs. 2 × 10 increasing to 3 × 15.
Exercise 11 Upright Rowing. 2 × 10 increasing to 3 × 15.
To get the best results, always warm up with **Exercises 1 to 8,** always cool down with **Exercises 7 and 8,** and follow the advice on diet in Chapters 4 to 6.

Your Schedule at a Leisure Centre
Basic all-round routine
Exercises 1 to 8 to warm up. 10 of each.
Exercise 57 Dead Lift. 2 × 10.
Exercise 61 Leg Squat. 2 × 10.
Exercise 63 Chinning. 2 × 10.
Exercise 55 Rowing. 2 × 10.
Exercise 52 Hip Flexor 2 × 10.
Exercise 58 Abdominal Conditioner Sit-ups. 2 × 10.
To this general schedule, add as required.

For Abdominals
Exercise 53 Thigh and Knee Leg Extension. 2 × 10 increasing to 3 × 15.
Exercise 64 Standing Twister. 2 × 10 increasing to 3 × 15.
On alternate weeks do **Exercise 65** Seated Twister instead.
Exercise 58 Abdominal Conditioner Sit-ups. Return to this and do 2 × 10 increasing to 3 × 15.

For Leg Development
Exercise 51 Leg Press. 2 × 10 increasing to 3 × 15.
Exercise 53 Thigh and Knee Leg Extension. 2 × 10 increasing to 3 × 15.
Exercise 56 Low Pulley Thigh Pulls. 2 × 10 increasing to 3 × 15.
Exercise 57 Dead Lift. 2 more sets of 2 × 10 increasing to 3 × 15.

For Arm Development
Exercise 54 High Pulley. 2 × 10 increasing to 3 × 15.
Exercise 59 Chest Press. 2 × 10 increasing to 3 × 15.
Exercise 62 Dipping. 2 × 10 increasing to 3 × 15.
Exercise 60 Chest Bench. 2 × 10 increasing to 3 × 15.

For Chest Development
Exercise 54 High Pulley. 2 × 10 increasing to 3 × 15.
Exercise 59 Chest Press. 2 × 10 increasing to 3 × 15.
Exercise 60 Chest Bench. 2 × 10 increasing to 3 × 15.
Exercise 62 Dipping. 2 × 10 increasing to 3 × 15.
Exercise 55 Rowing. Do another 2 × 10 increasing to 3 × 15.

You will realise that your range of exercises at a leisure centre is somewhat less than when working at home with barbell and dumb-bells, and hence the only thing you can do is to return to the muscles you are concentrating on and repeat the same exercises as you used in your general work-out. Again, it is important to always end with **Exercises 7 and 8** to cool down. 10 repetitions of each.

17 For Total Development

This chapter is for the serious body builder who wants all-over development, whether with a view to entering local or national body-building contests, or simply to become as well developed as she can be with her basic skeletal structure.

For this kind of improvement, it is necessary to take a long-term view. Muscles are not built in a day or even a month; you must think in terms of a year or two, hence the two-year course outlined below.

Train three nights a week with a night off in between. Work to the point of resistance in every set of exercises. (See Chapter 2.) Choose a weight that enables you to do 15 repetitions with an effort on the last one, for your first set. This number will drop to 12 perhaps on your second set and to 9 perhaps on your third set. When your strength has increased to the point where you are doing 18 on your first set, add a little weight to bring it back down to 15 again. Thus you will avoid lengthening your work-out to the point where it would take too long to complete.

One of the problems you will face with a two-year course is that you will become bored with doing the same exercises. To avoid this, change them every three months. You could just go on doing the ones you start with, week after week, but if you have enough apparatus available to make the changes it will help you to maintain your interest.

Your Schedule at Home
Months One to Three
Exercises 1 to 8 to warm up. 10 repetitions each.
Exercise 18(b) Quarter Squats with Barbell. 2 sets.

Exercise 15 Curls with Barbell. 2 sets.
Exercise 32 Triceps Stretch Standing. 2 sets.
Exercise 22 Good Morning Exercise with Barbell. 2 sets.
Exercise 10 Bent Over Rowing. 2 sets.
Exercise 13 Clean with Barbell. 2 sets.
Exercise 26 Straight Arm Pull-overs. 2 sets.
Exercise 23 Sit-ups with Weight. 2 sets.
Exercise 47 Leg Raises with Iron Boots from Prone Position. 2 sets.
Exercise 36 Side Bends with Dumb-bells. 2 sets.
Exercise 37 Trunk Turning with Dumb-bells. 2 sets.
Exercises 7 and 8 to relax. 10 repetitions each.

Months Four to Six
Exercises 1 to 8 to warm up. 10 repetitions each.
Exercise 18(a) Half Squats with Barbell. 3 sets.
Exercise 15 Curls with Barbell. 3 sets.
Exercise 16 Reverse Curls with Barbell. 3 sets.
Exercise 14 Press with Barbell. 3 sets.
Exercise 10 Bent Over Rowing. 3 sets.
Exercise 11 Upright Rowing. 3 sets.
Exercise 27 Bent Arm Pull-overs. 3 sets.
Exercise 23 Sit-ups with Weight. 3 sets.
Exercise 47 Leg Raises with Iron Boots from Prone Position. 3 sets.
Exercise 44 Iron Boots Knee Raises. 3 sets.
Exercise 43 Iron Boots Leg Swing. 3 sets.
Exercise 36 Side Bends with Dumb-bell. 3 sets.
Exercise 37 Trunk Turning with Dumb-bells. 3 sets.
Exercises 7 and 8 to relax. 10 repetitions each.

Months Seven to Nine
Exercises 1 to 8 to warm up. 10 repetitions each.
Exercise 18 Squats with Barbell. 3 sets.
Exercise 15 Curls with Barbell. 3 sets.
Exercise 33 Triceps Stretch Seated. 3 sets.
Exercise 17 Press Behind Neck with Barbell. 3 sets.
Exercise 31 Single Hand Rowing with Dumb-bell. 3 sets.
Exercise 23 Sit-ups with Weight. 3 sets.
Exercise 41 Iron Boots Leg Raise Sideways. 3 sets.
Exercise 42 Iron Boots Leg Raise Backwards. 3 sets.
Exercise 44 Iron Boots Knee Raises. 3 sets.
Exercise 43 Iron Boots Leg Swing. 3 sets.
Exercise 45 Iron Boots Thigh Extension. 3 sets.
Exercise 20 Heel Raises with Barbell. 3 sets.
Exercise 12 Bench Press. 3 sets.
Exercise 39 Side Bends with Dumb-bell Overhead. 3 sets.
Exercises 7 and 8 to relax. 10 repetitions each.

Months Ten to Twelve
Exercises 1 to 8 to warm up. 10 repetitions each.
Exercise 19 Squats with Barbell at Clean. 3 sets.
Exercise 21 Step-up onto Bench with Barbell. 3 sets.
Exercise 25 Crucifix with Dumb-bells. 3 sets.
Exercise 28 Alternate Dumb-bell Presses. 3 sets.
Exercise 29 Lateral Raises. 3 sets.
Exercise 30 Forwards and Upwards Swing with Dumb-bells. 3 sets.
Exercise 38 Squats with Dumb-bells at Shoulders. 3 sets.
Exercise 34 Single Arm Dumb-bell Curls. 3 sets.

Exercise 35 Dumb-bell Raises. 3 sets.
Exercise 46 Knee Raises with Iron Boots from Prone Position. 3 sets.
Exercise 48 Sit-ups with Weight on Incline Bench. 3 sets.
Exercise 14 Press with Barbell. 3 sets.
Exercise 12 Bench Press. 3 sets.
Exercises 7 and 8 to relax. 10 repetitions each.

After the first year, take a break for a couple of weeks, doing only **Exercises 1 to 8** to keep supple. Then, in your second year, repeat the first year's programme with the following variations:
1. Change the sequence each month instead of each quarter.
2. Do 4 sets of everything, instead of 3.

Your Schedule at a Leisure Centre
Start always with **Exercises 1 to 8** to warm up. 10 repetitions of each.
Then work round fourteen of the fifteen stations, leaving out **Exercise 65** one week and **Exercise 64** the next. These fifteen stations are designed to give you a complete work-out.
Cool down with **Exercises 7 and 8**. 10 repetitions each.

Months One to Four
Do 2 sets.

Months Five to Twelve
Do 3 sets.

In the Second Year
Do 4 sets.
Choose a resistance that enables you to do 15 repetitions on the first set, and increase it when you can do 18 on the first set.

To be most effective, this exercise programme must be combined with the diet in Chapter 6.

18 For Suppleness and Poise

Suppleness is achieved by exercising the joints gently so that the range of movement does not become restricted. Poise is achieved by knowing you are at your best, and acting with the quiet confidence that this knowledge breeds.

The enemies of suppleness are threefold:
1. Lack of regular exercise. If you sit about when your work is done, you will become stiff and then feel that you cannot exercise. This leads to further stiffening of the joints and you are in a vicious circle.
2. Overwork of one particular joint or limb. This happens if you have a purely repetitive job.
3. The ageing process. Do not think you have not got there yet. It starts as soon as you let yourself go.

For poise, the simple keep-fit routine in Chapter 14 may be all you need, though if you are self-conscious about any specific under-development, try the suggestions in Chapter 16, or if you know you are too fat, the slimming routines of Chapter 15.

For suppleness, you need full-range movement with very light weights. Use dumb-bells of 5lb or even lighter if these seem too heavy to handle easily. Exercise three nights a week, with a day off between.

Your Schedule at Home

Exercises 1 to 8 to warm up. 10 repetitions each.
Exercise 28 Alternate Dumb-bell Presses. 30 each hand.
Exercise 29 Lateral Raises. 30.
Exercise 30 Forwards and Upwards Swing with Dumb-bells. 30 each hand.
Exercise 35 Dumb-bell Raises. 30 each hand.
Exercise 36 Side Bends with Dumb-bells. 30 each side.
Exercise 37 Trunk Turning with Dumb-bells. 30 each way.
Exercise 43 Leg Swing, but without iron boots. 20 each leg.
Exercise 23 Sit-ups but without weight. 20 increasing to 30.
Exercise 47 Leg Raises from Prone Position but without iron boots. 30 each leg.
Exercises 7 and 8 to cool down. 10 repetitions of each.

Try to perform the above exercises smoothly and rhythmically, and at no time use a weight bigger than you can easily handle.

Your Schedule at a Leisure Centre

Exercises 1 to 8 to warm up. 10 repetitions each.
Exercise 52 Hip Flexor. 15.
Exercise 54 High Pulley. 15.
Exercise 55 Rowing. 15.
Exercise 56 Low Pulley Thigh Pulls. 15.
Exercise 58 Abdominal Conditioner Sit-ups. 15.
Exercise 62 Dipping. 10.
Exercise 63 Chinning. 10.
Exercise 64 Standing Twister. 15.
Exercise 65 Seated Twister. 15.
Exercises 7 and 8 to cool down. 10 repetitions of each.

Where weights are involved in the above machine exercises, use very light resistances that you can easily manage or you may develop bulging muscles that will make you even less supple.

19 For Stamina

One of the best methods of training for stamina is circuit training. It also promotes all-round health. Circuit training was first expounded by R.E. Morgan and G.T. Adamson in their book *Circuit Training*, published by G. Bell and Sons Ltd in 1957. Since that date it has become very popular with athletes whatever their chosen sport or event.

The basic idea of circuit training is that you have ten exercises which you arrange in such an order that no two similar muscle groups are exercised consecutively. For example, a leg exercise must be followed by an arm exercise or an abdominal exercise. Having chosen your exercises, you lay out the apparatus ready. Choosing fairly light weights, you find the score of how many repetitions of each exercise you can perform in sixty seconds, resting if you need. You record these scores, and then you halve them to get the number you are actually going to perform.

The training then consists of starting at the beginning of the circuit and working round three times, doing these half-scores. You must complete three circuits with little or no rest at all. It should take approximately thirty minutes. When you have improved to the stage where it is only taking you twenty minutes, you re-test yourself as you did in the beginning, and get a new series of half-scores, which makes the circuit that much harder, and will probably take your time back to thirty minutes again.

If, after a few months, you find your scores are getting too high, add a little weight to bring them down again, but never work with heavy weights. The circuit is sometimes made up of entirely free-standing exercises which use no apparatus, but cir-cuits using weights are detailed below.

There are three advantages to this system:
1 The exercises are continuously varied, which adds interest.
2 The time taken is short, only thirty minutes.
3 The exercises can be done in a confined space.

There is no time to stop and change weights on bar or dumb-bell rod, so you must select a weight low enough for you to do the hardest exercise fairly easily. You can set up any circuit to please yourself, and if you do not have enough apparatus you can fill in with some exercises that do not need apparatus. Make sure, however, that your scheme covers every muscle group in the body; it should never concentrate on just one group. Train two nights a week if you are aiming to improve your stamina for some sport, and do the circuit training instead of other weight training not in addition to it, though you can of course do the training demanded by your particular sport on the other nights.

Keep records of your progress so that you are not continuously thinking about what weight you should be using.

Your Schedule at Home
Exercise 18 Squats with Barbell.
Exercise 14 Press with Barbell.
Exercise 23 Sit-ups with Weight.
Exercise 19 Squats with Barbell at Clean.
Exercise 15 Curls with Barbell.
Exercise 47 Leg Raises with Iron Boots from Prone Position.
Exercise 11 Upright Rowing.
Exercise 21 Step-up onto Bench with Barbell.
Exercise 27 Bent Arm Pull-overs.

Exercise 44 Iron Boots Knee Raises.

You will know enough about weight training by now to see that this exercises all muscle groups, and that no group is exercised twice in succession. You can of course adapt the circuit to the apparatus available.

If you train in a leisure centre, you may find that they already have a circuit, and that one student will start at the beginning, and as he moves on to the next piece of apparatus, the others will follow him round. If, at your particular centre, they do not use circuit training as a method, you may have difficulty in moving on, as other people may be using the equipment you need at that particular moment. However, if you can train there, the following is a suggested sequence.

Your Schedule at a Leisure Centre

Exercise 61 Leg Squat.

Exercise 59 Chest Press.

Exercise 58 Abdominal Conditioner Sit-ups.

Exercise 56 Low Pulley Thigh Pulls.

Exercise 62 Dipping.

Exercise 52 Hip Flexor.

Exercise 53 Thigh and Knee Leg Extension.

Exercise 63 Chinning.

Exercise 64 Standing Twister.

Exercise 55 Rowing.

Again, you can set up any alternative circuit to suit your specific needs, providing you stick to the basic principles of the method.

20 For Special Conditions

Weight training can be undertaken for remedial purposes, for example to strengthen a joint after a fracture, to rebuild a muscle after a long stay in bed, to increase mobility in a limb, but these are such specialised cases that it is impossible to deal with them in a book of this nature, and you should be guided by your doctor or physiotherapist.

Women often wonder, however, whether exercise can be taken during pregnancy. Today, doctors generally agree that since pregnancy is not an illness women can carry on normal physical activity, and this can include exercise unless specifically forbidden by a doctor. There is no evidence to suggest that taking such exercise is going to benefit your unborn child, but the benefit to your own health will have an indirect effect.

Exercise during pregnancy should be regular and gentle, and if you feel any discomfort you should stop. Most weight-training instructors would say that if you are already doing weight training, you can continue as long as you are able, using very light weights. But all are agreed that it is not the time to start if you have not been doing any regular training. Swimming or walking would be a more sensible alternative.

Your Schedule at Home
Exercise 1 Deep Knee Bends. 10 repetitions.
Exercise 3 Trunk Turning. 20 each side.
Exercise 4 Side Bends. 20 each side.
Exercise 6 Touching Alternate Toes. 20 each side.
Exercise 7 Deep Breathing with Arms Swinging. 2 × 10.
Exercise 9 Back Exercise. 10 repetitions.
The last named is especially good for backache during pregnancy.

You will note that no apparatus has been used, but if you want to add some dumbbell exercises, do:
Exercise 29 Lateral Raises. 10 with a maximum of 5lb.
Exercise 30 Forwards and Upwards Swing with Dumb-bells. 10 with 5lb.
The above should keep you fit, but if you have any doubts as to the benefit, consult your doctor.

After the baby has been born and a suitable interval has elapsed, you will want exercises that are helpful in restoring your figure. Again, be guided by your doctor, but the following course should help:
Exercises 1 to 8 to warm up. 10 repetitions each.
Exercise 23 Sit-ups but without using a weight. 10 increasing to 25.
Exercise 24 Trunk Turning with Bar on Shoulders. No weight on bar. 10 each side.
Exercise 36 Side Bends with Dumb-bells. 10 each side.
Exercise 11 Upright Rowing. 10 increasing to 20.
Exercise 26 Straight Arm Pull-overs. 2 × 10.
Exercise 41 Leg Raise Sideways but without iron boots. 10 each leg.
Exercise 43 Leg Swing without iron boots. 10 each leg.
Exercise 44 Knee Raises without iron boots. 10 each leg.
Exercise 46 Knee Raises from Prone Position without iron boots. 10 increasing to 20.
Exercise 47 Leg Raises from Prone Position without iron boots. 10 increasing to 20.
Exercises 7 and 8 to cool down. 10 repetitions each.
Do not try to do more than you can comfort-

ably manage, and only start after you have fully recovered and have been given the 'all clear' by your doctor.

It is most unlikely that the Instructor at a leisure centre would accept you as a beginner whilst you were pregnant, and it would be most unwise to train there on your own, so a course is not included here.

After the baby has been born, and with the same provisos as the above home course, you would find the following schedule helpful:

Exercises 1 to 8 to warm up. 10 repetitions of each.

Exercise 52 Hip Flexor. 10 to 15 repetitions.

Exercise 58 Abdominal Conditioner Sit-ups. 10 to 15.

Exercise 62 Dipping. 10 to 20.

Exercise 64 Standing Twister. 10 to 20.

Exercise 63 Chinning. 10 to 20.

Exercise 54 High Pulley. 10 to 15.

Start with the lower number of repetitions given and work up to the higher figure over a month or two. Use weights that you can easily manage and, only when you have fully recovered, consider any of the courses in the other chapters of this section.

21 For Athletics

The value of weight training in aiding athletic performance only began to receive recognition in Britain after the 1952 Olympics, though it was accepted in America and on the continent of Europe before that. Today most top athletes supplement their preparation with weight training.

There are three ways in which weight training can help:

1   By increasing general fitness and strength.
2   By developing stamina.
3   By building up the muscles specifically needed for your event.

Since concentration on any muscle group should always be within the framework of an all-round training, you should follow the schedule for General Fitness (Chapter 14) or for Stamina (Chapter 19), adding the exercises from this chapter that are needed for your specific activity. Some of these will, of course, be repeating exercises you have just done, but they will give extra work to the muscles you use.

As in previous chapters alternative programmes are given for those working at home or in a leisure centre. Wherever you are training, train twice a week, on nights when you are not doing your athletic training. Always warm up with 10 each of **Exercises 1 to 8**. Always cool down with 10 each of **Exercises 7 and 8**.

Running
You need stamina, good legs and good lungs. To your schedule at home, add:
Exercise 41 Iron Boots Leg Raise Sideways. 2 × 10 increasing to 3 × 10.
Exercise 42 Iron Boots Leg Raise Backwards. 2 × 10 increasing to 3 × 10.
Exercise 45 Iron Boots Thigh Extension. 2 × 10 increasing to 3 × 10.
Exercise 18(a) Half Squats with Barbell. 2 × 10 increasing to 3 × 10.
Exercise 20 Heel Raises with Barbell. 2 × 10 increasing to 3 × 10.

To your schedule at a leisure centre, add:
Exercise 51 Leg Press. 2 × 10 increasing to 3 × 10.
Exercise 53 Thigh and Knee Leg Extension. 2 × 10 increasing to 3 × 10.
Exercise 56 Low Pulley Thigh Pulls. 2 × 10 increasing to 3 × 10.
Exercise 61 Leg Squat. 2 × 10 increasing to 3 × 10.
Exercise 55 Rowing. 2 × 10 increasing to 3 × 10.

Hurdling
You need the same muscles as runners, plus spring and co-ordination.
To your schedule at home, add:
All the above exercises for runners plus
Exercise 21 Step-up onto Bench with Barbell. 2 × 10 increasing to 3 × 10.
Exercise 23 Sit-ups with Weight. 2 × 10 increasing to 3 × 10.

To your schedule at a leisure centre, add:
All the above exercises for runners plus
Exercise 58 Abdominal Conditioner Sit-ups. 2 × 10 increasing to 3 × 10.
Exercise 52 Hip Flexor. 2 × 10 increasing to 3 × 10.

High Jump
You need good leg muscles, agility and supple hips.
To your schedule at home, add:
Exercise 18 Squats with Barbell. 2 × 10 increasing to 3 × 10.

Exercise 20 Heel Raises with Barbell. 2 × 10 increasing to 3 × 10.
Exercise 43 Iron Boots Leg Swing. 2 × 10 increasing to 3 × 10.
Exercise 22 Good Morning Exercise with Barbell. 2 × 10 increasing to 3 × 10.
Exercise 36 Side Bends with Dumb-bells. 2 × 10 increasing to 3 × 10.
Exercise 37 Trunk Turning with Dumb-bells. 2 × 10 increasing to 3 × 10.

To your schedule at a leisure centre, add:
Exercise 61 Leg Squat. 2 × 10 increasing to 3 × 10.
Exercise 51 Leg Press. 2 × 10 increasing to 3 × 10.
Exercise 56 Low Pulley Thigh Pulls. 2 × 10 increasing to 3 × 10.
Exercise 55 Rowing. 2 × 10 increasing to 3 × 10.
Exercise 64 Standing Twister. 2 × 10 increasing to 3 × 10.

Long Jump
You need good leg muscles and supple hips, plus speed for the run up and the take off.
To your schedule at home, add:
All the above exercises for the high jump plus
Exercise 21 Step-up onto Bench with Barbell. 2 × 10 increasing to 3 × 10.

To your schedule at a leisure centre, add:
All the above exercises for the high jump plus
Exercise 53 Thigh and Knee Leg Extension. 2 × 10 increasing to 3 × 10.

Pole Vault
You need arm, shoulder and abdominal development, spring and co-ordination.
To your schedule at home, add:
Exercise 15 Curls with Barbell. 2 × 10 increasing to 3 × 10.
Exercise 16 Reverse Curls with Barbell. 2 × 10 increasing to 3 × 10.
Exercise 12 Bench Press. 2 × 10 increasing to 3 × 10.
Exercise 18 Squats with Barbell. 2 × 10 increasing to 3 × 10.
Exercise 11 Upright Rowing. 2 × 10 increasing to 3 × 10.
Exercise 44 Iron Boots Knee Raises. 2 × 10 increasing to 3 × 10.

Exercise 23 Sit-ups with Weight. 2 × 10 increasing to 3 × 10.
Exercise 14 Press with Barbell. 2 × 10 increasing to 3 × 10.

To your schedule at a leisure centre, add:
Exercise 54 High Pulley. 2 × 10 increasing to 3 × 10.
Exercise 59 Chest Press. 2 × 10 increasing to 3 × 10.
Exercise 62 Dipping. 2 × 10 increasing to 3 × 10.
Exercise 63 Chinning. 2 × 10 increasing to 3 × 10.
Exercise 61 Leg Squat. 2 × 10 increasing to 3 × 10.
Exercise 58 Abdominal Conditioner Sit-ups. 2 × 10 increasing to 3 × 10.
Exercise 52 Hip Flexor. 2 × 10 increasing to 3 × 10.

Javelin
You need strong shoulders, hip, abdominal and leg development.
To your schedule at home, add:
Exercise 11 Upright Rowing. 2 × 10 increasing to 3 × 10.
Exercise 17 Press Behind Neck with Barbell. 2 × 10 increasing to 3 × 10.
Exercise 26 Straight Arm Pull-overs. 2 × 10 increasing to 3 × 10.
Exercise 27 Bent Arm Pull-overs. 2 × 10 increasing to 3 × 10.
Exercise 35 Dumb-bell Raises. 2 × 10 increasing to 3 × 10.
Exercise 39 Side Bends with Dumb-bell Overhead. 2 × 10 increasing to 3 × 10.

To your leisure centre schedule, add:
Exercise 54 High Pulley. 2 × 10 increasing to 3 × 10.
Exercise 59 Chest Press. 2 × 10 increasing to 3 × 10.
Exercise 62 Dipping. 2 × 10 increasing to 3 × 10.
Exercise 60 Chest Bench. 2 × 10 increasing to 3 × 10.
Exercise 63 Chinning. 2 × 10 increasing to 3 × 10.

Discus
You need especially the oblique abdominals and hip and leg development.
To your schedule at home, add:

Exercise 39 Side Bends with Dumb-bell Overhead. 2 × 10 increasing to 3 × 10.
Exercise 24 Trunk Turning with Bar on Shoulders. 2 × 10 increasing to 3 × 10.
Exercise 29 Lateral Raises. 2 × 10 increasing to 3 × 10.
Exercise 30 Forwards and Upwards Swing with Dumb-bells. 2 × 10 increasing to 3 × 10.

To your schedule at a leisure centre, add:
Exercise 52 Hip Flexor. 2 × 10 increasing to 3 × 10.
Exercise 64 Standing Twister. 2 × 10 increasing to 3 × 10.
Exercise 58 Abdominal Conditioner Sit-ups. 2 × 10 increasing to 3 × 10.
Exercise 57 Dead Lift. 2 × 10 increasing to 3 × 10.

Shot Put
This needs overall strength.
To your schedule at home, add:
Exercise 18 Squats with Barbell. 2 × 10 increasing to 3 × 10.
Exercise 12 Bench Press. 2 × 10 increasing to 3 × 10.
Exercise 17 Press Behind Neck with Barbell. 2 × 10 increasing to 3 × 10.
Exercise 28 Alternate Dumb-bell Presses. 2 × 10 increasing to 3 × 10.
Exercise 39 Side Bends with Dumb-bell Overhead. 2 × 10 increasing to 3 × 10.
Exercise 40 Wrist Roller Exercise. 3 increasing to 4.

To your schedule at a leisure centre, add:
Exercise 61 Leg Squat. 2 × 10 increasing to 3 × 10.
Exercise 60 Chest Bench. 2 × 10 increasing to 3 × 10.
Exercise 59 Chest Press. 2 × 10 increasing to 3 × 10.
Exercise 52 Hip Flexor. 2 × 10 increasing to 3 × 10.
Exercise 57 Dead Lift. 2 × 10 increasing to 3 × 10.
Exercise 63 Chinning. 2 × 10 increasing to 3 × 10.

Once you are experienced with this type of training you can reduce the number of exercises you do and concentrate on the particular ones you feel that you personally need, but for the first few months at least you should do the full range. When you reduce the number of different exercises you perform, you can increase the number of sets to 4, rather than increase the weight used.

22 For Sports

As with athletics, if you are using weight training to help you with a sport, train twice a week, alternating your weight-training and your sports-training nights. Use light weights; do the sets indicated, never to the point of resistance. Add the exercises in this chapter to either the schedule for General Fitness (Chapter 14) or for Stamina (Chapter 19). Although you will be repeating some of the exercises you have just done, they will give extra work to the muscles you especially want to develop.

As before, alternative schedules are given for those working at home or in a leisure centre.

Badminton
You need strong wrists, speed, good reflexes and strong leg and back muscles.

To your schedule at home, add:
Exercise18(a) Half Squats with Barbell. 3 × 10.
Exercise 21 Step-up onto Bench with Barbell. 3 × 10.
Exercise 26 Straight Arm Pull-overs. 3 × 10.
Exercise 34 Single Arm Dumb-bell Curls. 3 × 10.
Exercise 40 Wrist Roller Exercise. 3 repetitions.
Exercise 30 Forwards and Upwards Swing with Dumb-bells. 3 × 10.

To your schedule at a leisure centre, add:
Exercise 61 Leg Squat. 3 × 10.
Exercise 54 High Pulley. 3 × 10.
Exercise 63 Chinning. 3 × 10.
Exercise 56 Low Pulley Thigh Pulls. 3 × 10.
Exercise 65 Seated Twister. 3 × 10.

Cycling
You need good leg and back muscles and stamina. Circuit training (Chapter 19) would be best.

To your schedule at home, add:
Exercise 18 Squats with Barbell. 3 × 10.
Exercise 20 Heel Raises with Barbell. 3 × 10.
Exercise 44 Iron Boots Knee Raises. 3 × 10.
Exercise 45 Iron Boots Thigh Extension. 3 × 10.
Exercise 25 Crucifix with Dumb-Bells. 3 × 10.
Exercise 12 Bench Press. 3 × 10.
Exercise 29 Lateral Raises. 3 × 10.
Exercise 26 Straight Arm Pull-overs. 3 × 10.

To your leisure centre schedule, add:
Exercise 51 Leg Press. 3 × 10.
Exercise 61 Leg Squat. 3 × 10.
Exercise 53 Thigh and Knee Leg Extension. 3 × 10.
Exercise 56 Low Pulley Thigh Pulls. 3 × 10.
Exercise 55 Rowing. 3 × 10.
Exercise 54 High Pulley. 3 × 10.
Exercise 57 Dead Lift. 3 × 10.
Exercise 58 Abdominal Conditioner Sit-ups. 3 × 10.

Fencing
You need leg power, arm and hip development and strong wrists.

To your schedule at home, add:
Exercise 21 Step-up onto Bench with Barbell. 3 × 10.
Exercise 38 Squats with Dumb-bells at

Shoulders. 3 × 10.

Exercise 31 Single Hand Rowing with Dumb-bell. 3 × 10.

Exercise 37 Trunk Turning with Dumbbells. 3 × 10.

Exercise 40 Wrist Roller Exercise. 3 repetitions.

Exercise 39 Side Bends with Dumb-bell Overhead. 3 × 10.

To your leisure centre schedule, add:

Exercise 51 Leg Press. 3 × 10.

Exercise 53 Thigh and Knee Leg Extension. 3 × 10.

Exercise 59 Chest Press. 3 × 10.

Exercise 52 Hip Flexor. 3 × 10.

Exercise 60 Chest Bench. 3 × 10.

Exercise 54 High Pulley. 3 × 10.

Exercise 63 Chinning. 3 × 10.

Golf

You need strong shoulders and supple hips.

To your schedule at home, add:

Exercise 11 Upright Rowing. 3 × 10.

Exercise 17 Press Behind Neck with Barbell. 3 × 10.

Exercise 29 Lateral Raises. 3 × 10.

Exercise 39 Side Bends with Dumb-bell Overhead. 3 × 10.

Exercise 24 Trunk Turning with Bar on Shoulders. 3 × 10.

To your schedule at a leisure centre, add:

Exercise 54 High Pulley. 3 × 10.

Exercise 57 Dead Lift. 3 × 10.

Exercise 52 Hip Flexor. 3 × 10.

Exercise 63 Chinning. 3 × 10.

Exercise 64 Standing Twister. 3 × 10.

Hockey

You need leg and hip exercises, speed and stamina.

To your schedule at home, add:

Exercise 38 Squats with Dumb-bells at Shoulders. 3 × 10.

Exercise 41 Leg Raise Sideways without iron boots. 3 × 10.

Exercise 42 Leg Raise Backwards without iron boots. 3 × 10.

Exercise 45 Iron Boots Thigh Extension. 3 × 10.

Exercise 39 Side Bends with Dumb-bell Overhead. 3 × 10.

To your schedule at a leisure centre, add:

Exercise 61 Leg Squats. 3 × 10.

Exercise 56 Low Pulley Thigh Pulls. 3 × 10.

Exercise 53 Thigh and Knee Leg Extension. 3 × 10.

Exercise 52 Hip Flexor. 3 × 10.

Exercise 58 Abdominal Conditioner Sit-ups. 3 × 10.

Netball

You need arm and leg muscles, fitness and speed.

To your schedule at home, add:

Exercise 18 Squats with Barbell. 3 × 10.

Exercise 43 Leg Swing without iron boots. 3 × 10.

Exercise 26 Straight Arm Pull-overs. 3 × 10.

Exercise 27 Bent Arm Pull-overs. 3 × 10.

Exercise 28 Alternate Dumb-bell Presses. 3 × 10.

To your schedule at a leisure centre, add:

Exercise 61 Leg Squat. 3 × 10.

Exercise 56 Low Pulley Thigh Pulls. 3 × 10.

Exercise 59 Chest Press. 3 × 10.

Exercise 54 High Pulley. 3 × 10.

Squash

You need speed, fitness, wrist, arm, back and leg muscles. Very light weights and high repetitions are the best plan.

To your schedule at home, add:

Exercise 40 Wrist Roller Exercise. 3 repetitions.

Exercise 26 Straight Arm Pull-overs. 3 × 12.

Exercise 29 Lateral Raises. 3 × 12.

Exercise 33 Triceps Stretch Seated. 3 × 12.

Exercise 34 Single Arm Dumb-bell Curls. 3 × 12.

Exercise 43 Leg Swing without iron boots. 3 × 12.

Exercise 22 Good Morning Exercise with Barbell. 3 × 12.

To your schedule at a leisure centre, add:
Exercise 54 High Pulley. 3 × 12.
Exercise 63 Chinning. 3 × 12.
Exercise 56 Low Pulley Thigh Pulls. 3 × 12.
Exercise 52 Hip Flexor. 3 × 12.
Exercise 55 Rowing. 3 × 12.
Exercise 61 Leg Squat. 3 × 12.

Swimming
You need good lungs, arm power, legs and back muscles.

To your schedule at home, add:
Exercise 12 Bench Press. 3 × 10.
Exercise 15 Curls with Barbell. 3 × 10.
Exercise 16 Reverse Curls with Barbell. 3 × 10.
Exercise 11 Upright Rowing. 3 × 10.
Exercise 44 Iron Boots Knee Raises. 3 × 10.

To your schedule at a leisure centre, add:
Exercise 59 Chest Press. 3 × 10.
Exercise 57 Dead Lift. 3 × 10.
Exercise 63 Chinning. 3 × 10.
Exercise 55 Rowing. 3 × 10.
Exercise 60 Chest Bench. 3 × 10.

Tennis
You need good wrist, shoulder, leg and back muscles.

To your schedule at home, add:
Exercise 26 Straight Arm Pull-overs. 3 × 10.
Exercise 40 Wrist Roller Exercise. 3 repetitions.
Exercise 22 Good Morning Exercise with Barbell. 3 × 10.
Exercise 29 Lateral Raises. 3 × 10.
Exercise 35 Dumb-bell Raises. 3 × 10.
Exercise 24 Trunk Turning with Bar on Shoulders. 3 × 10.
Exercise 18 Squats with Barbell. 3 × 10.

To your schedule at a leisure centre, add:
Exercise 54 High Pulley. 3 × 10.
Exercise 63 Chinning. 3 × 10.
Exercise 64 Standing Twister. 3 × 10.
Exercise 60 Chest Bench. 3 × 10.
Exercise 61 Leg Squat. 3 × 10.
Exercise 55 Rowing. 3 × 10.
Exercise 62 Dipping. 3 × 10.

When you are fully experienced you can reduce the number of exercises to those you particularly need personally, and at the same time you can increase either the number of repetitions or the number of sets or both. Try, however, to keep some balance in your programme, and remember that heavy weights will develop strength but may slow you down; light weights and high repetitions give speed and suppleness.

Index